# ローマ字［ヘボン式］



| | | | | | | | | |
|---|---|---|---|---|---|---|---|---|
| | ア a | イ i | ウ u | エ e | オ o | | | |
| k | カ ka | キ ki | ク ku | ケ ke | コ ko | キャ kya | キュ kyu | キョ kyo |
| s | サ sa | シ shi | ス su | セ se | ソ so | シャ sha | シュ shu | ショ sho |
| t | タ ta | チ chi | ツ tsu | テ te | ト to | チャ cha | チュ chu | チョ cho |
| n | ナ na | ニ ni | ヌ nu | ネ ne | ノ no | ニャ nya | ニュ nyu | ニョ nyo |
| h | ハ ha | ヒ hi | フ fu | ヘ he | ホ ho | ヒャ hya | ヒュ hyu | ヒョ hyo |
| m | マ ma | ミ mi | ム mu | メ me | モ mo | ミャ mya | ミュ myu | ミョ myo |
| y | ヤ ya | — | ユ yu | — | ヨ yo | | | |
| r | ラ ra | リ ri | ル ru | レ re | ロ ro | リャ rya | リュ ryu | リョ ryo |
| w | ワ wa | — | — | — | — | | | |
| n | ン n | | | | | | | |
| g | ガ ga | ギ gi | グ gu | ゲ ge | ゴ go | ギャ gya | ギュ gyu | ギョ gyo |
| z | ザ za | ジ ji | ズ zu | ゼ ze | ゾ zo | ジャ ja | ジュ ju | ジョ jo |
| d | ダ da | ヂ ji | ヅ zu | デ de | ド do | | | |
| b | バ ba | ビ bi | ブ bu | ベ be | ボ bo | ビャ bya | ビュ byu | ビョ byo |
| p | パ pa | ピ pi | プ pu | ペ pe | ポ po | ピャ pya | ピュ pyu | ピョ pyo |

- 「ん」はnで表しますが，p，b，mの前ではmを使います。 shimbun（新聞）
- 「っ」はその次の文字を重ねて書きます。 gakko（学校）

# New ABC of ENGLISH

## 単語編

by
SAICHI IIZUKA

SOEISHA

# もくじ

## この本の特長と使い方

- 子ども達にとって身近なことばから，興味のあることばまで約700語を集めました。単語を暗記するのではなく，基本的な英文にあてはめて練習しながら，自然に単語が身につけられるようになっています。
- この本にはネイティブスピーカーによるCDが付いています。まず絵を見ながらCDを数回聞かせ，次に英語の意味を説明しながら発音の練習をさせます。そのあと英文にあてはめて練習をさせましょう。
- この本には指導用マニュアルが付いています。指導用マニュアルには，指導者向けに文法的な説明もされていますが，子ども達が英語を楽しく学習できるように，子ども達に文法的な説明をすることは避けましょう。

- 2ページで1レッスンになっています。各レッスンの終わりには，楽しみながら聞きとりの確認学習ができる，LET'S TRY!のコーナーがあります。問題の英文はCDに収録されています。
- CDのトラック番号は，レッスンの番号と対応しています。CDには，英単語や英文が，本に付けられた①～の番号順に収録されています。
- 本には，単語に青い字でa，an，theが付いているものがありますが，CDにはa，an，theは収録されていません。

# Lesson 1 The alphabet アルファベット

① Aa

② Bb

③ Cc

④ Dd

⑤ Ee

⑥ Ff

⑦ Gg

⑧ Hh

⑨ Ii

⑩ Jj

⑪ Kk

⑫ Ll

⑬ Mm

⑭ Nn

⑮ Oo

## LET'S SING

# The ABC Song

# Lesson 2 Food 食べ物

① bread

② butter

③ jam

④ hamburger

⑤ hot dog

⑥ French fries

⑦ sandwich

⑧ pizza

⑨ ham and eggs

⑩ cheese

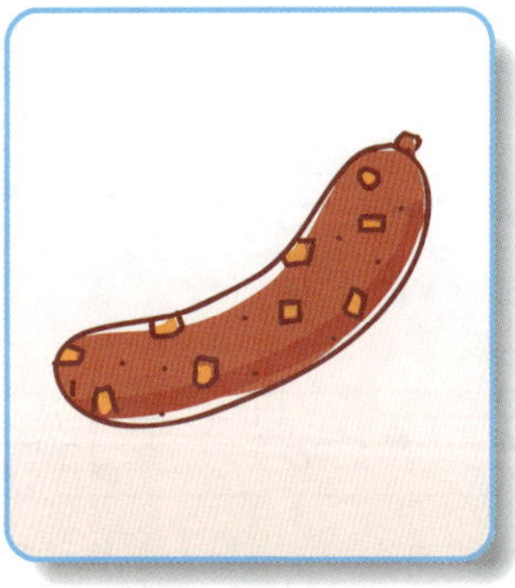

⑪ sausage

⑫ soup

⑬ steak

⑭ pasta

⑮ curry and rice

⑯ stew

⑰ salad

⑱ rice

⑲ beef

⑳ pork

㉑ chicken

㉒ fish

## LET'S TRY

どの食べ物のことかな。

# Lesson 3 Dessert and Drink デザートと飲み物

① candy

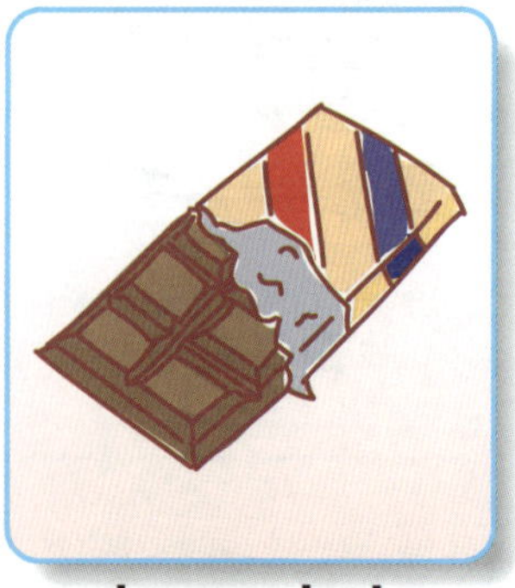
② chocolate

③ gum

④ potato chips

⑤ popcorn

⑥ donut

⑦ apple pie

⑧ cake

⑨ cream puff

⑩ cookie

⑪ pudding

⑫ yogurt

⑬ ice cream

⑭ soft ice cream

⑮ sherbet

⑯ cola

⑰ juice

⑱ shake

⑲ milk

⑳ coffee

㉑ tea

㉒ cocoa

㉓ green tea

㉔ water

## LET'S TRY

どのデザートのことかな。

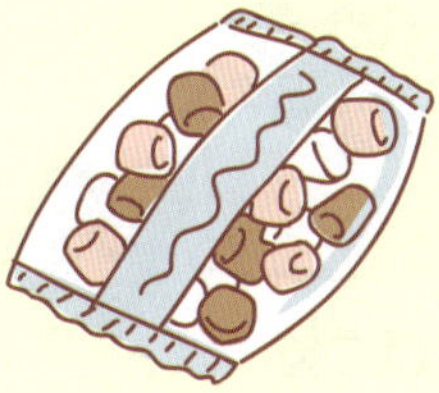

# Lesson 4 Colors and Shapes 色と形

① white

② yellow

③ orange

④ green

⑤ purple

⑥ pink

⑦ red

⑧ brown

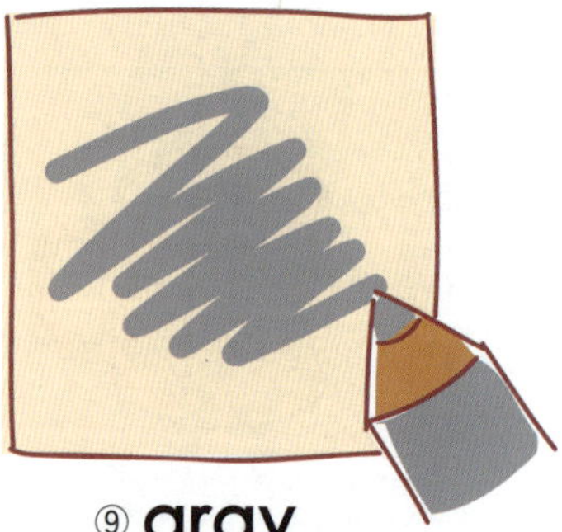

⑨ gray

⑩ black

⑪ blue

⑫ a star

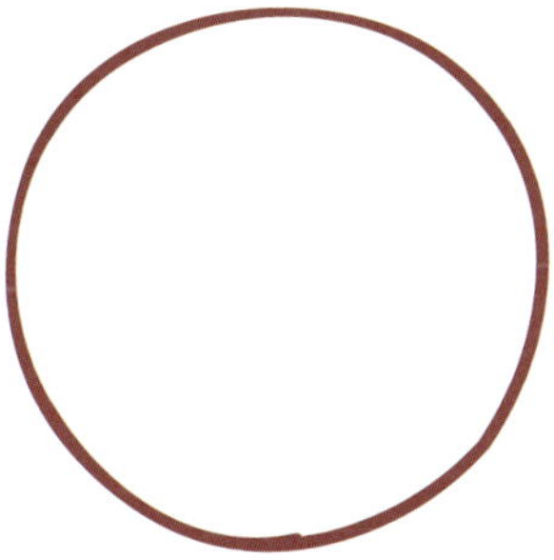

⑬ a circle

⑭ a triangle

⑮ a square

⑯ a rectangle

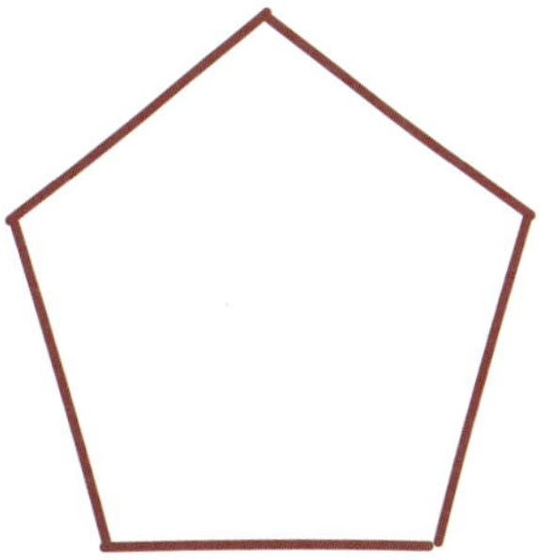

⑰ a pentagon

⑱ a ring

⑲ a heart

⑳ a diamond

㉑ a yellow ring

㉒ a blue diamond

## LET'S TRY

あう形をえらびましょう。

## Lesson 5 My face and body わたしの顔と体

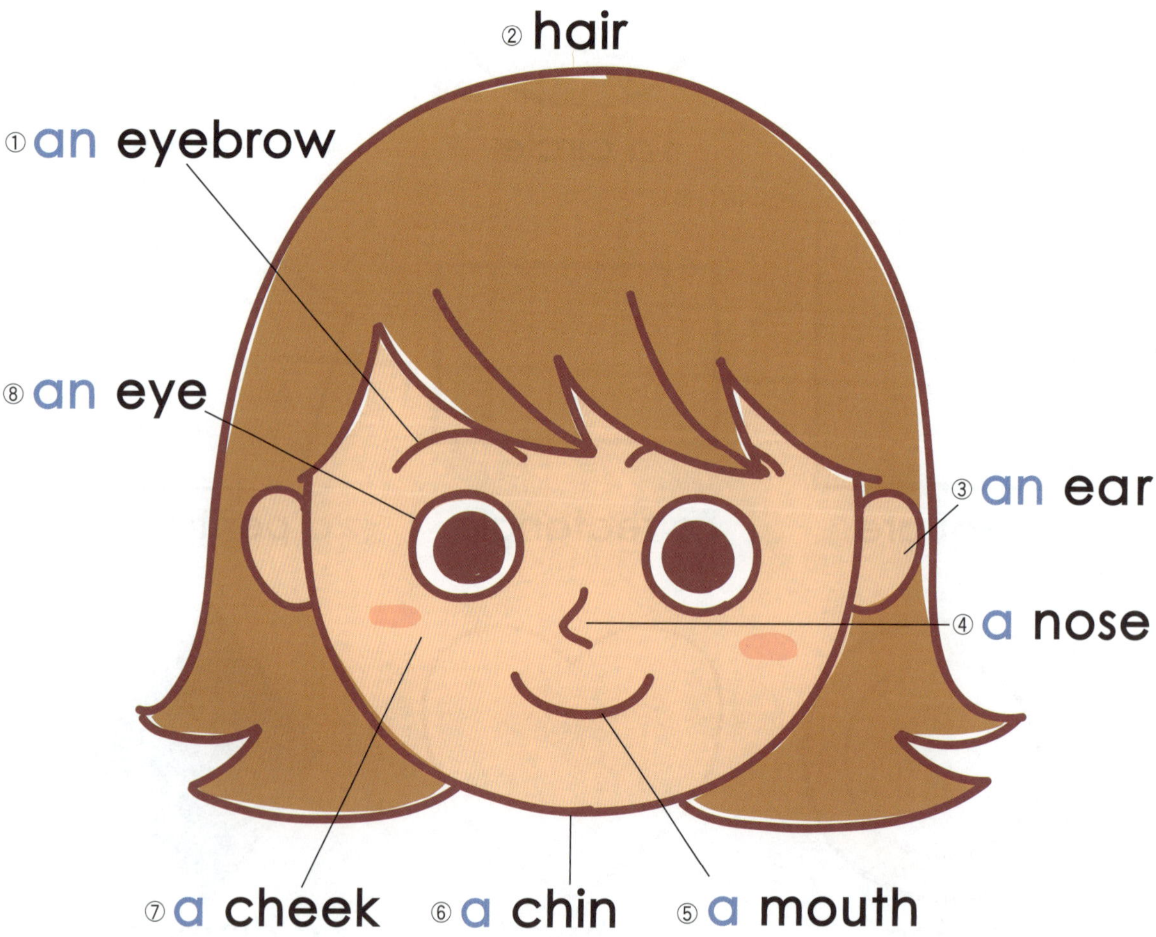


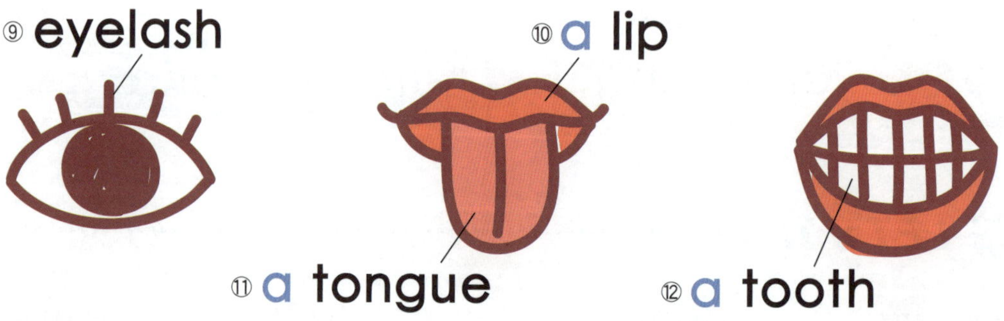

㉜
Touch your ear, Ken.

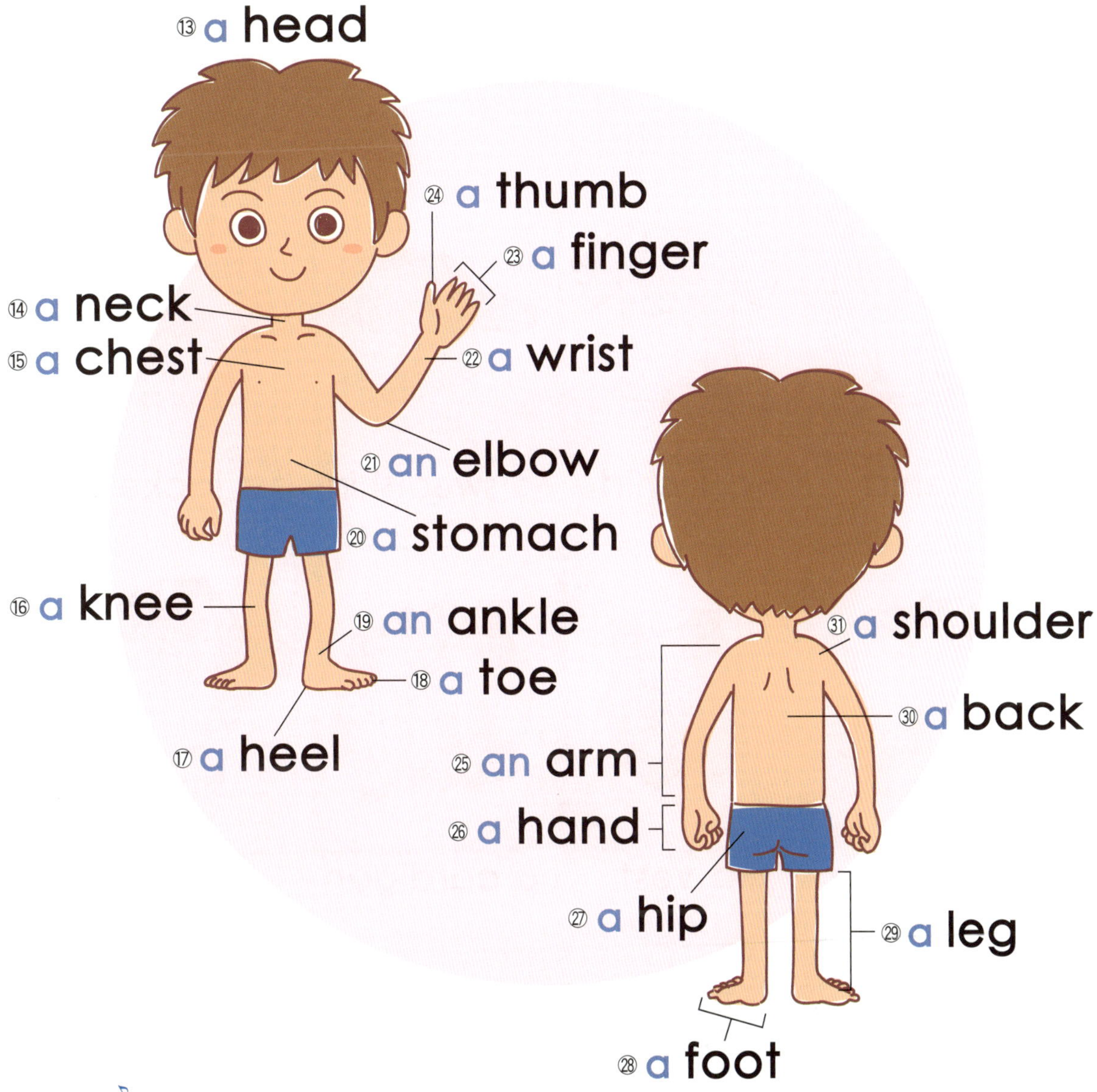


## LET'S TRY

正しくできているのはどの子かな。

1

2

# Lesson 6 Clothing 身(み)につけるもの

① a shirt

② a T-shirt

③ a sweatshirt

④ a jacket

⑤ a sweater

⑥ a vest

⑦ a cardigan

⑧ a suit

⑨ jeans

⑩ pants

⑪ a skirt

⑫ a wedding dress

⑬ an apron

⑭ pajamas

⑮ a raincoat

⑯ a uniform

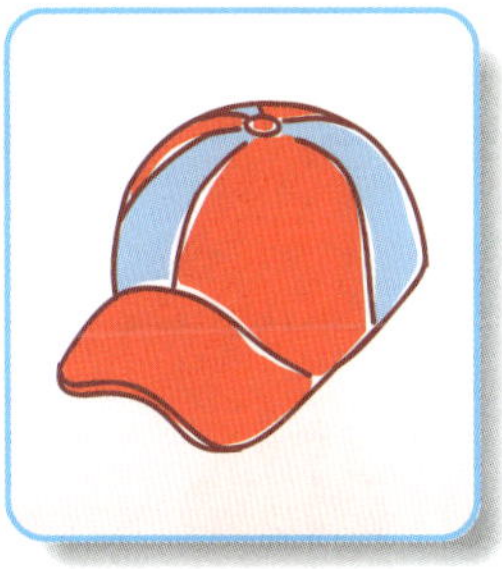

⑰ a cap

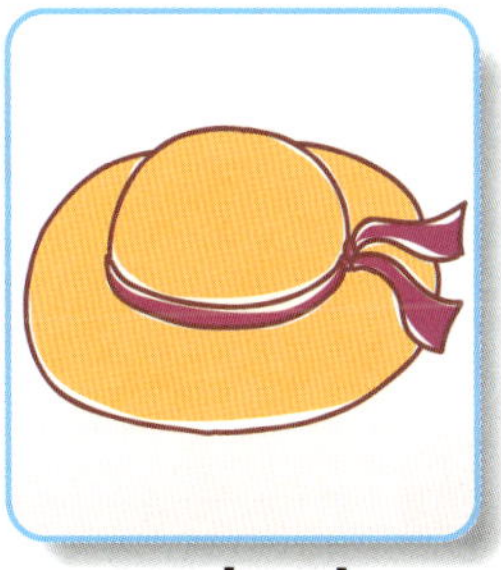

⑱ a hat

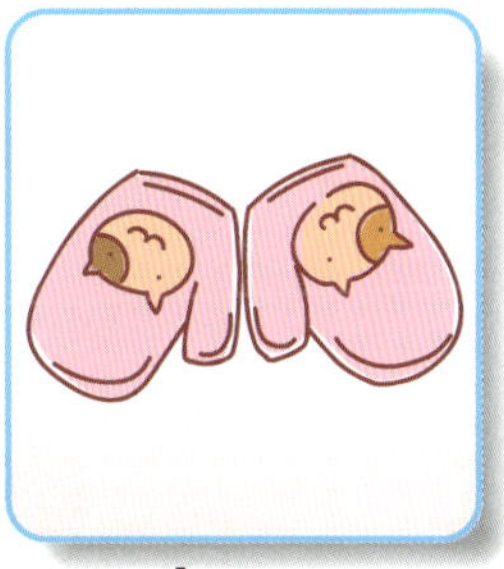

⑲ gloves

⑳ a scarf

㉑ a belt

㉒ a tie

㉓ a ring

㉔ glasses

㉕ a handkerchief

㉖ socks

㉗ shoes

㉘ rain boots

㉙ Touch your pink T-shirt, Rika.

## LET'S TRY

どれのことかな。

# Lesson 7 Stand up, please. 立(た)ってください。

① walk

② run

③ jump

④ skip

⑤ turn

⑥ stop

⑦ stand up

⑧ sit down

⑨ clap

⑲
Stand up, please.

⑩ open a window

⑪ shut a door

⑫ cook

⑬ catch a ball

⑭ throw a ball

⑮ call

⑯ sing

⑰ dance

⑱ fly

## LET'S TRY

あう絵をえらびましょう。

# Lesson 8 Numbers 数（かず）

①

| 1 | 2 | 3 | 4 | 5 | 6 |
|---|---|---|---|---|---|
| one | two | three | four | five | six |

② a sweater　③ vests　④ cardigans

⑧ aprons　⑨ hats　⑩ caps

⑭

How old are you?

I am eight years old.

| 7 | 8 | 9 | 10 | 11 | 12 |
| --- | --- | --- | --- | --- | --- |
| seven | eight | nine | ten | eleven | twelve |

## LET'S TRY

あう絵をえらびましょう。

# Lesson 9 The world せかい

㉑
Where are you from?

I'm from Brazil.

⑳ My name is Mira.
I'm from India.

⑰ Canada

⑱ The United States

⑲ Brazil

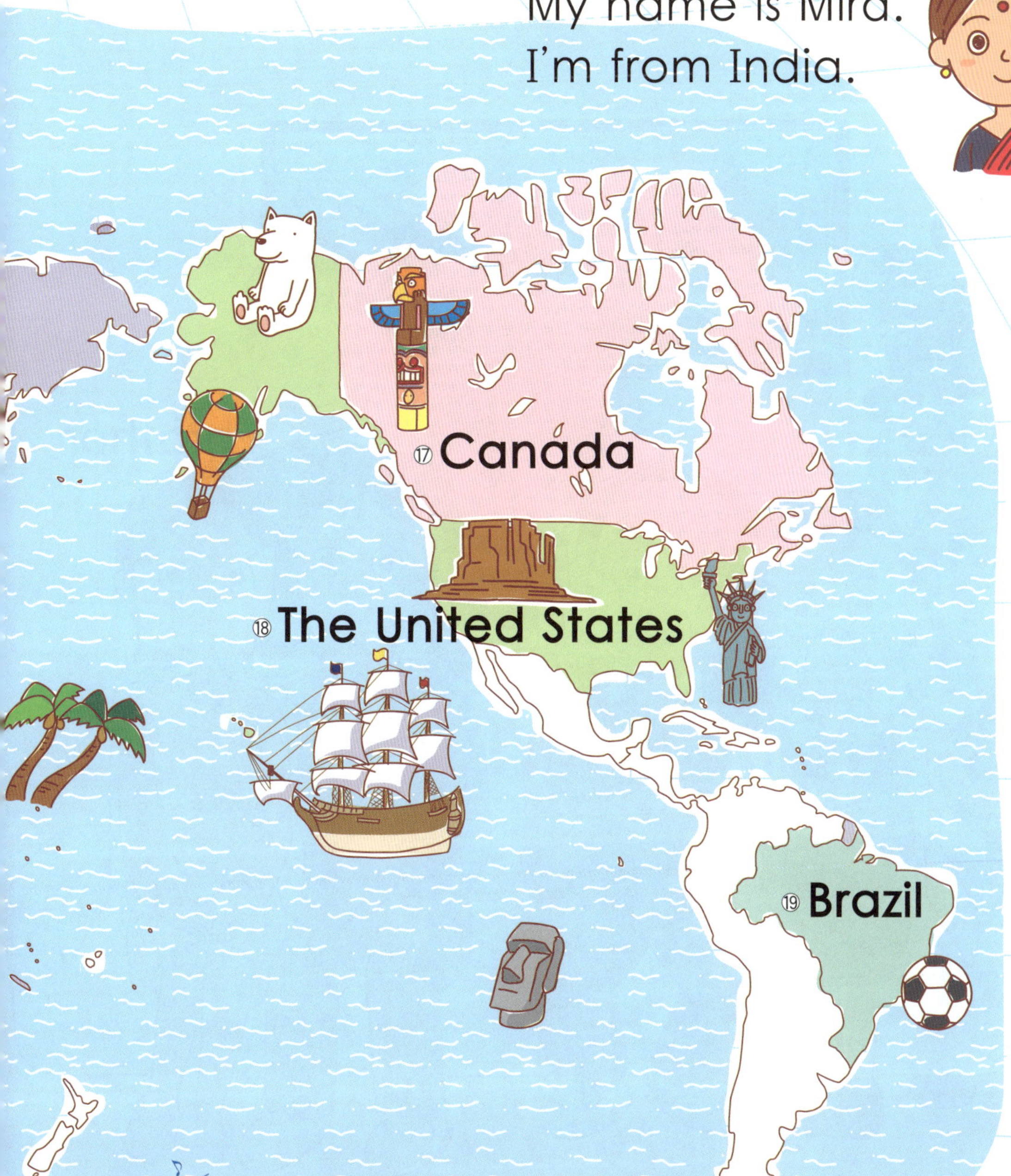

## LET'S TRY

あう絵をえらびましょう。

# Lesson 10 My family わたしの家族（かぞく）

⑮ This is my brother, Akira.
And this is my sister, Sayaka.

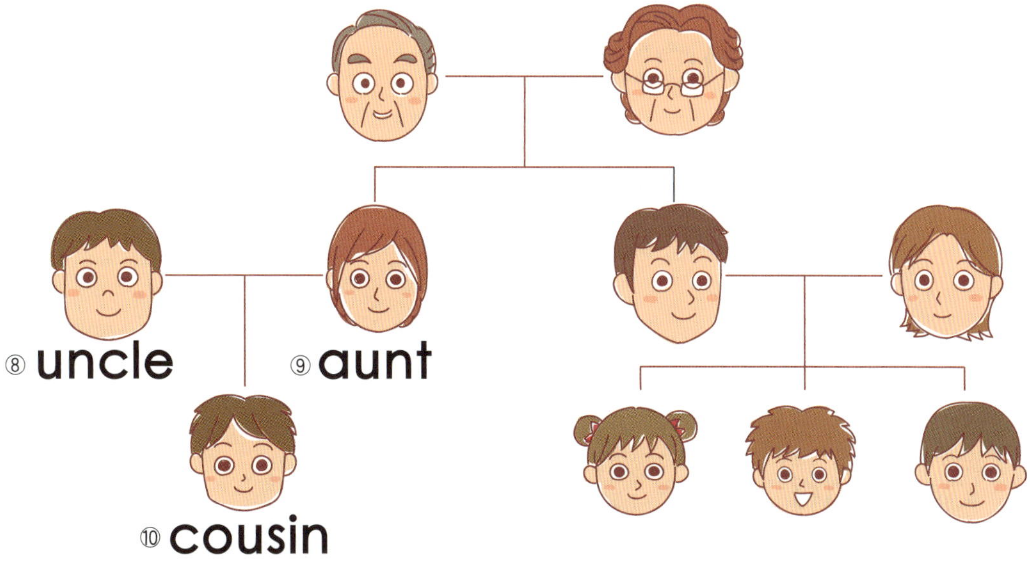

⑯

Who is this?　　It is my cousin, Naoto.

## LET'S TRY

あう写真をえらびましょう。

# Lesson 11 Our house わたしたちの家(いえ)

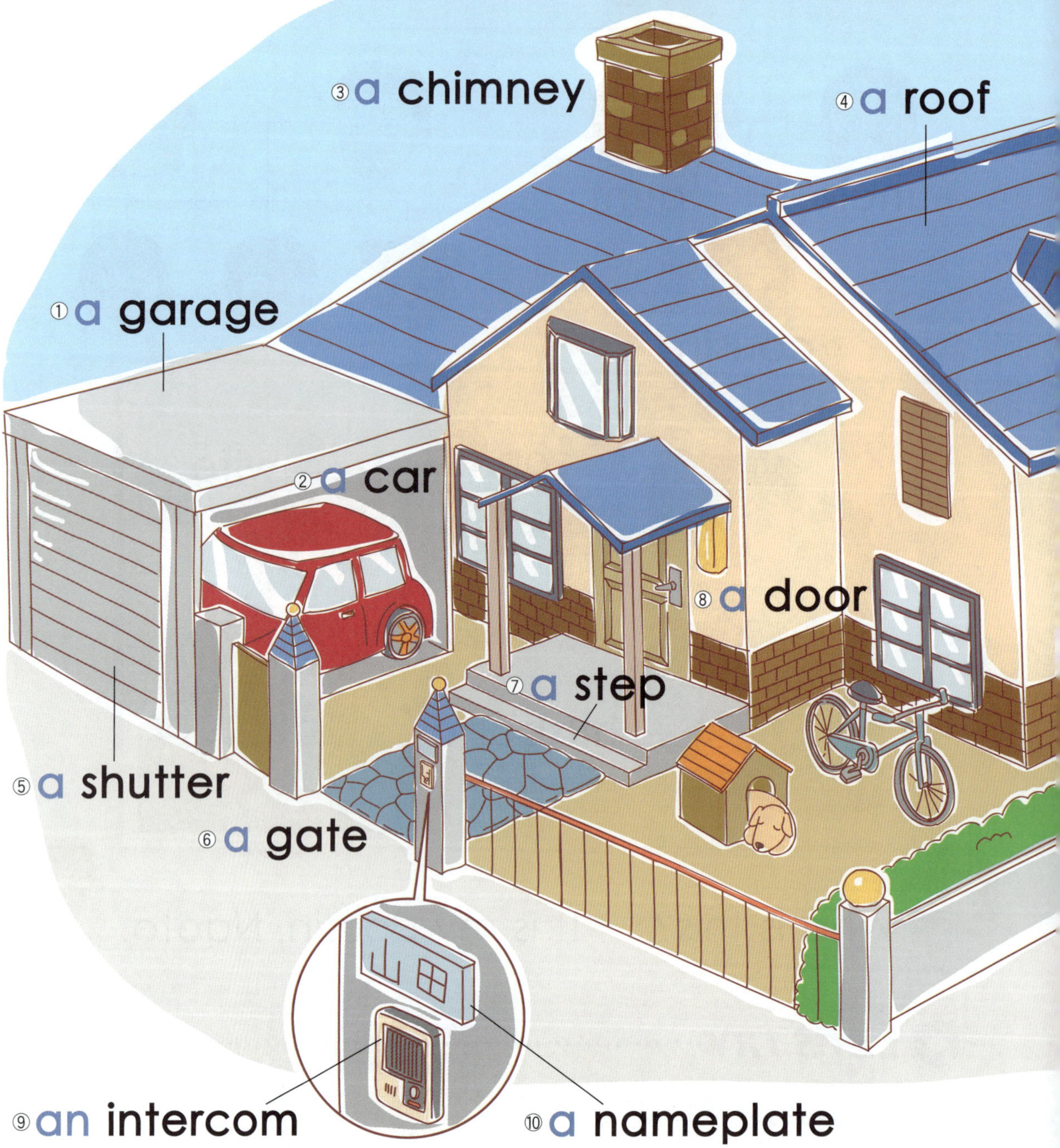

## LET'S TRY

あう絵をえらびましょう。

# Lesson 12 In our house わたしたちの家の中

① an entrance

② stairs

③ a dining room

④ a kitchen

⑤ a living room

⑥ a bedroom

⑦ a bathroom

⑧ a toilet

⑨ Is this a bathroom?

Yes, it is.

# In our bathroom

㉑ Is that your shampoo?　　No, it is not.

## LET'S TRY

あう絵をえらびましょう。

# Lesson 13 Our living room わたしたちの居間

㉒ What is this? It's a light.

## LET'S TRY

あう絵をえらびましょう。

# Lesson 14 Our kitchen わたしたちの台所(だいどころ)

㉓
This isn't my cup.
It's my brother's.

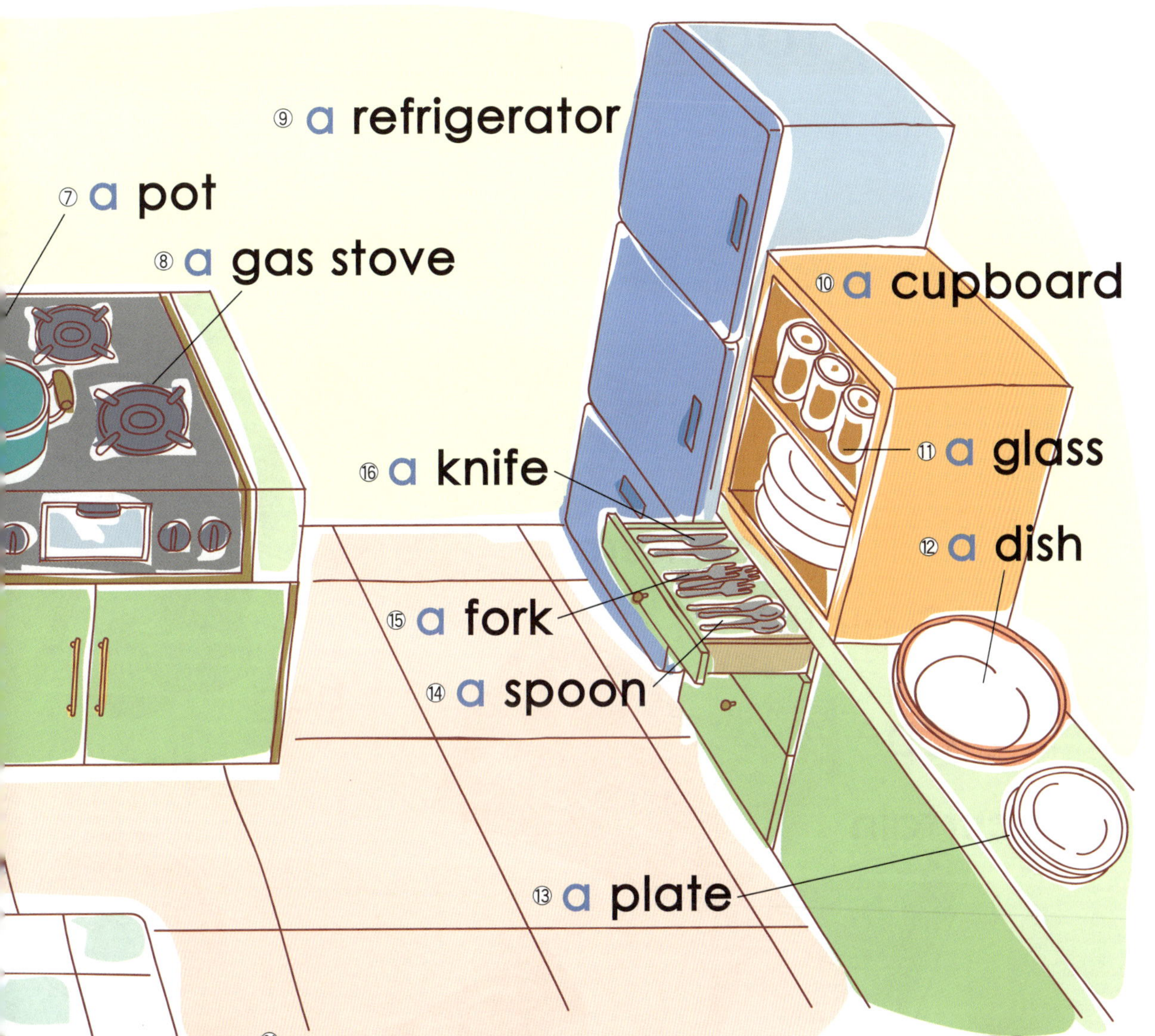

㉔ Whose plate is this?

It's mine.

## LET'S TRY

あう絵をえらびましょう。

# Lesson 15 My room わたしの部屋

⑳ Where is my glove? It's in the bag.

㉑

Where is my bat?

It's on the chair.

Where are my balls, then?

They are under the chair.

## LET'S TRY

あうほうの絵をえらびましょう。

# Lesson 16 In the country いなか

⑮
Where is your favorite place?
It's an amusement park.

## LET'S TRY

あう絵をえらびましょう。

# Lesson 17 In the town 町の中

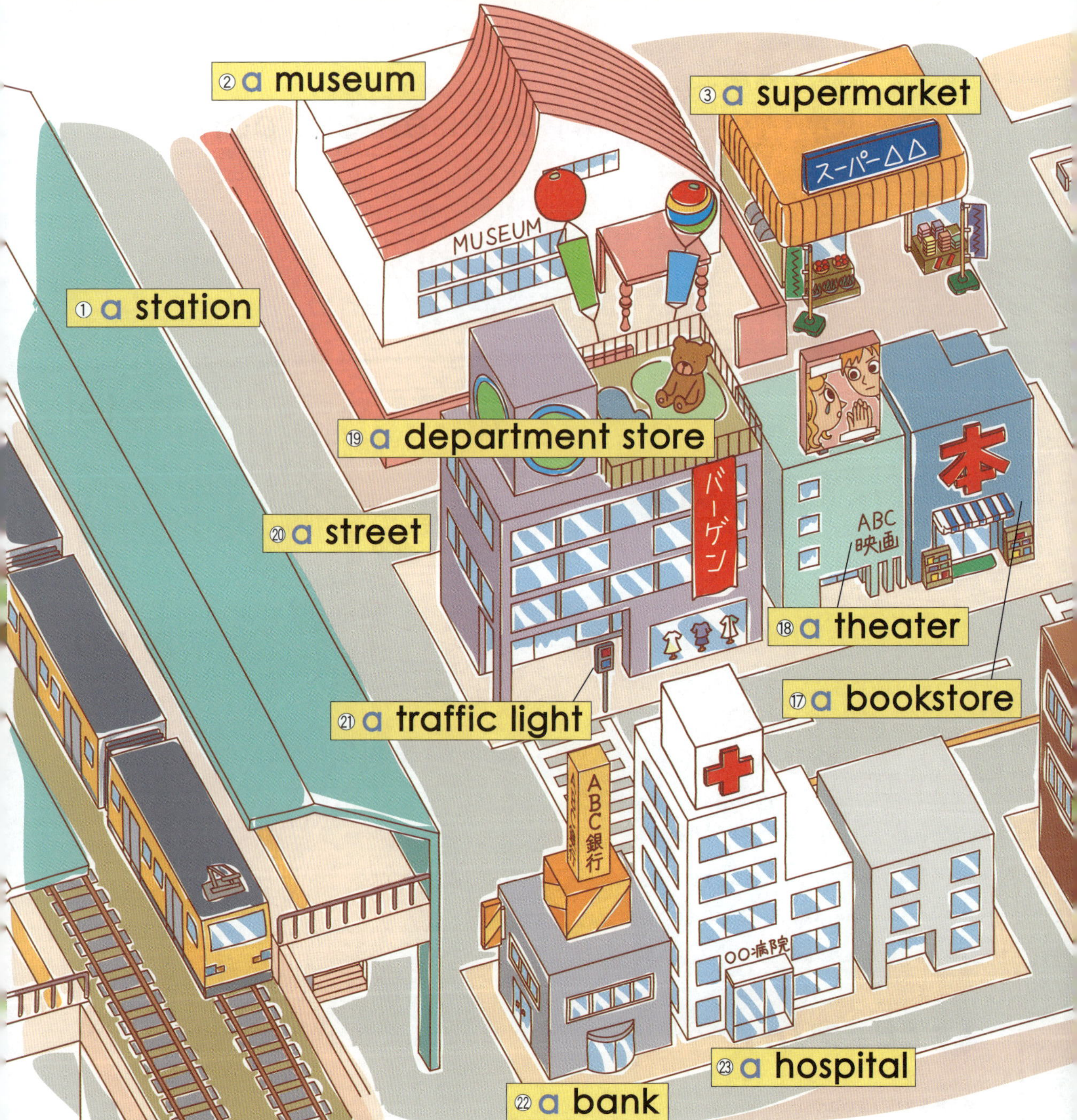


㉔

Where is a bank?

It's next to the hospital.

Where is a museum?

It's in front of the station.

## LET'S TRY

あうほうの絵をえらびましょう。

# Lesson 18 Fruits くだもの

① apple

② banana

③ orange

④ cherry

⑤ strawberry

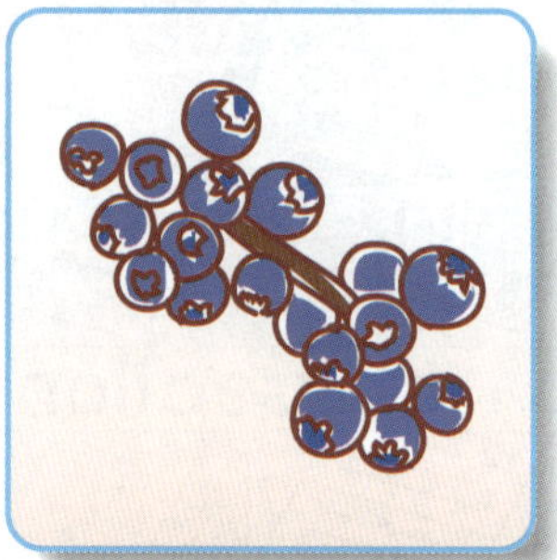

⑥ blueberry

⑦ grapes

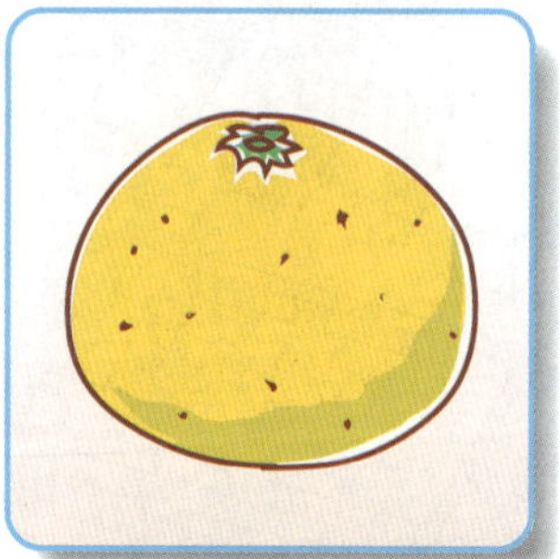

⑧ grapefruit

⑨ lemon

⑩ melon

⑪ watermelon

⑫ peach

㉒
I like apples.

⑬ fig

⑭ pear

⑮ persimmon

⑯ kiwi

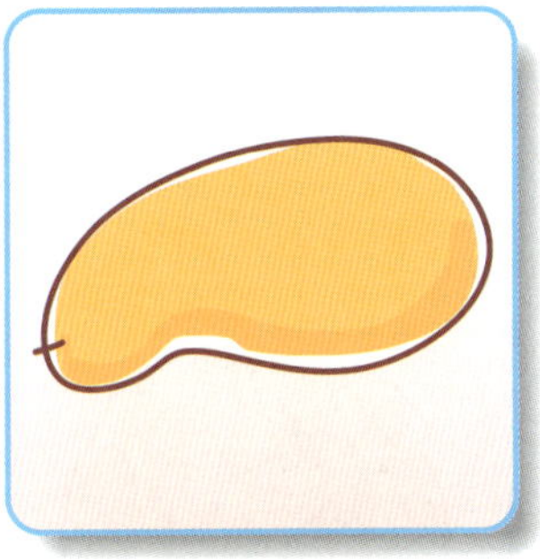
⑰ mango

⑱ pineapple

⑲ chestnut

⑳ walnut

㉑ coconut

㉓
I do not like bananas.

## LET'S TRY

あう絵をえらびましょう。

# Lesson 19 Vegetables　やさい

① carrot

② onion

③ potato

④ cucumber

⑤ lettuce

⑥ tomato

⑦ cabbage

⑧ celery

⑨ corn

⑩ green pepper

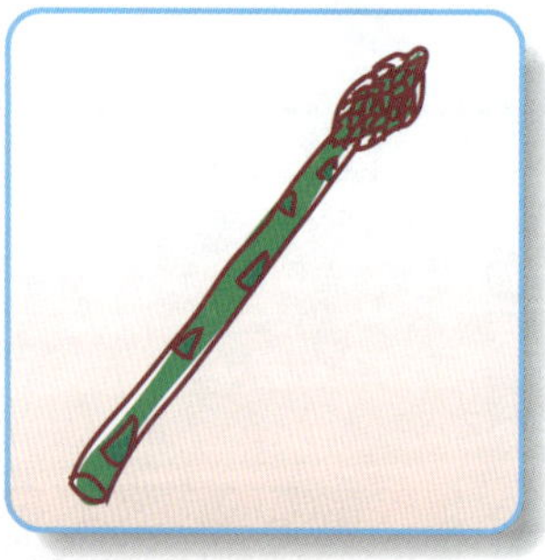

⑪ asparagus

⑫ broccoli

㉕

Do you like carrots?

Yes, I do.

⑬ parsley

⑭ radish

⑮ pumpkin

⑯ spinach

⑰ turnip

⑱ beans

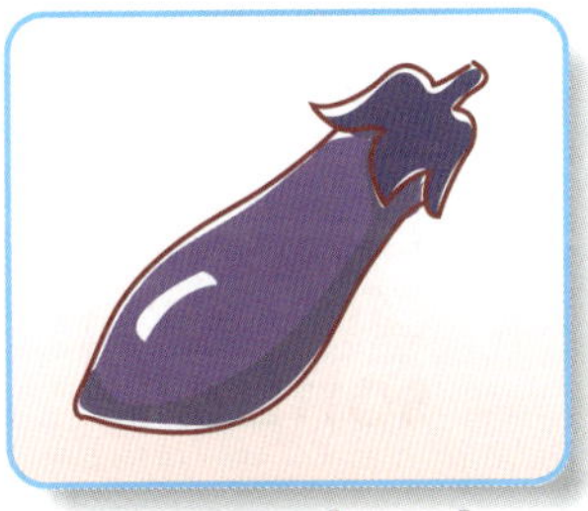

⑲ eggplant

⑳ okra

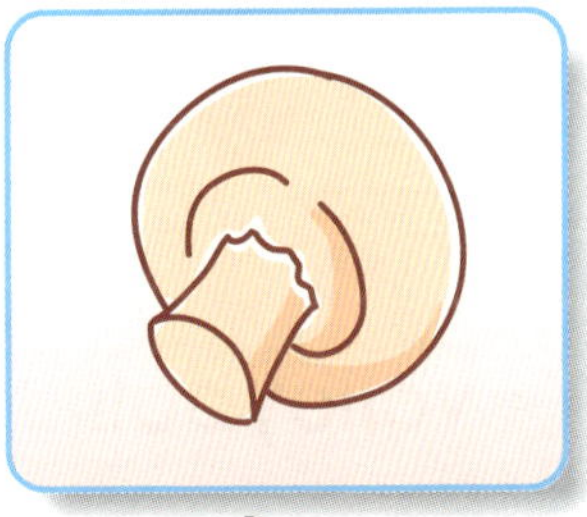

㉑ mushroom

㉒ garlic

㉓ ginger

㉔ leek

㉖

Do you like leeks?

No, I don't.

## LET'S TRY

あう絵をえらびましょう。

# Lesson 20 Sports スポーツ

① baseball

② basketball

③ soccer

④ volleyball

⑤ rugby

⑥ softball

⑦ badminton

⑧ tennis

⑨ table tennis

⑩ gymnastics

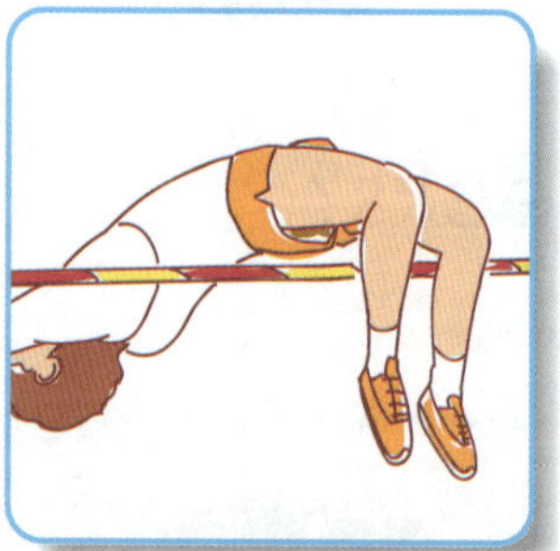

⑪ the high jump

⑫ marathon

⑬ track and field

㉓

My sister likes tennis.
She often plays tennis.

⑭ **weight lifting**

⑮ **boxing**

⑯ **golf**

⑰ **bowling**

⑱ **skating**

⑲ **skiing**

⑳ **skateboarding**

㉑ **surfing**

㉒ **swimming**

㉔

My brother plays soccer well.

But he does not play baseball very well.

## LET'S TRY

あう絵をえらびましょう。

# Lesson 21 Instruments 楽器

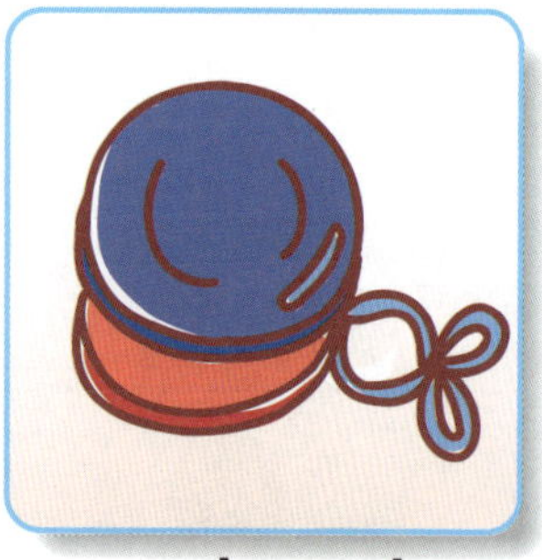

① castanets

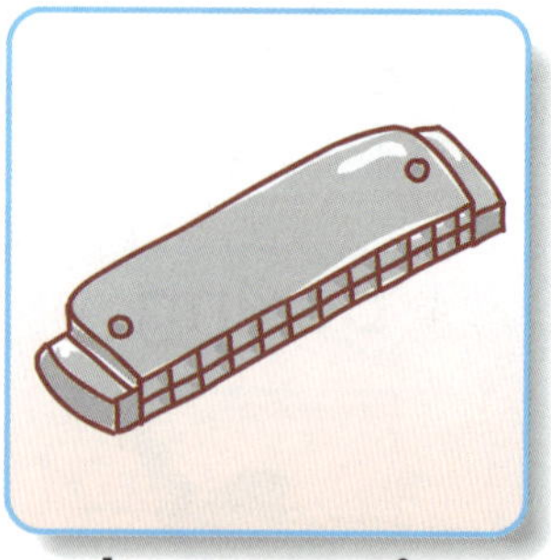

② a harmonica

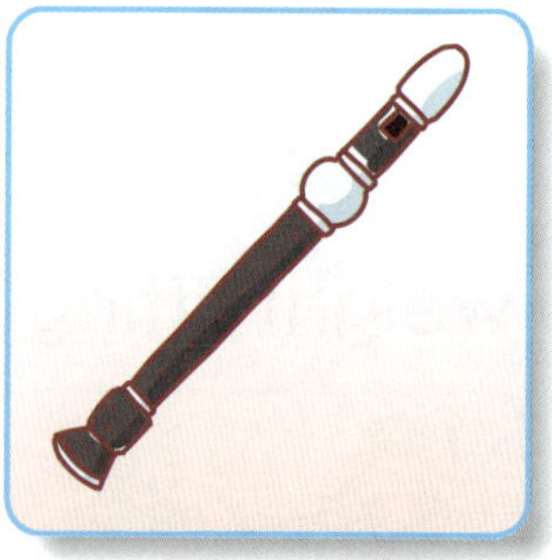

③ a recorder

④ cymbals

⑤ a tambourine

⑥ a triangle

⑦ a piano ⑧ a violin ⑨ a cello ⑩ a bass

⑳ Does your mother play the piano?

Yes, she does.

⑪ **drums**

⑫ a **guitar**

⑬ a **saxophone**

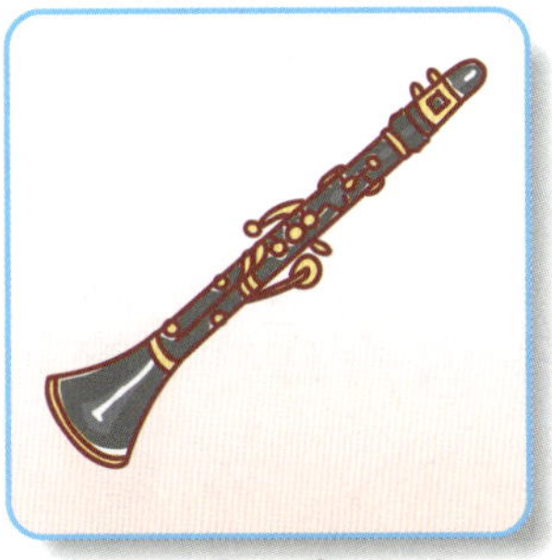

⑭ a **clarinet**

⑮ a **flute**

⑯ a **trumpet**

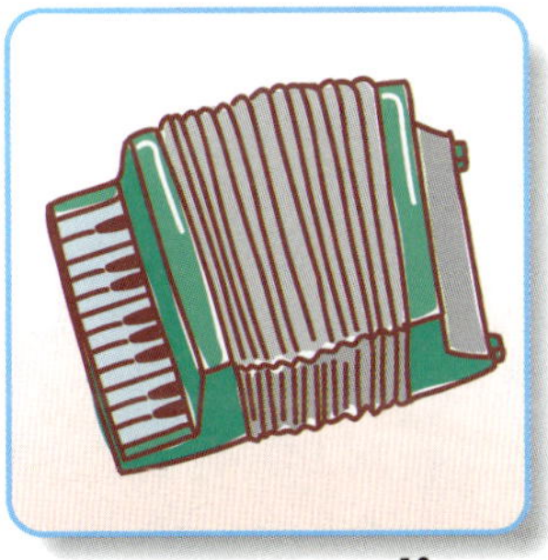

⑰ an **accordion**

⑱ a **xylophone**

⑲ a **harp**

㉑
Does your father play the guitar?

No, he doesn't.

## LET'S TRY

あう絵をえらびましょう。

# Lesson 22 Our elementary school わたしたちの小学校

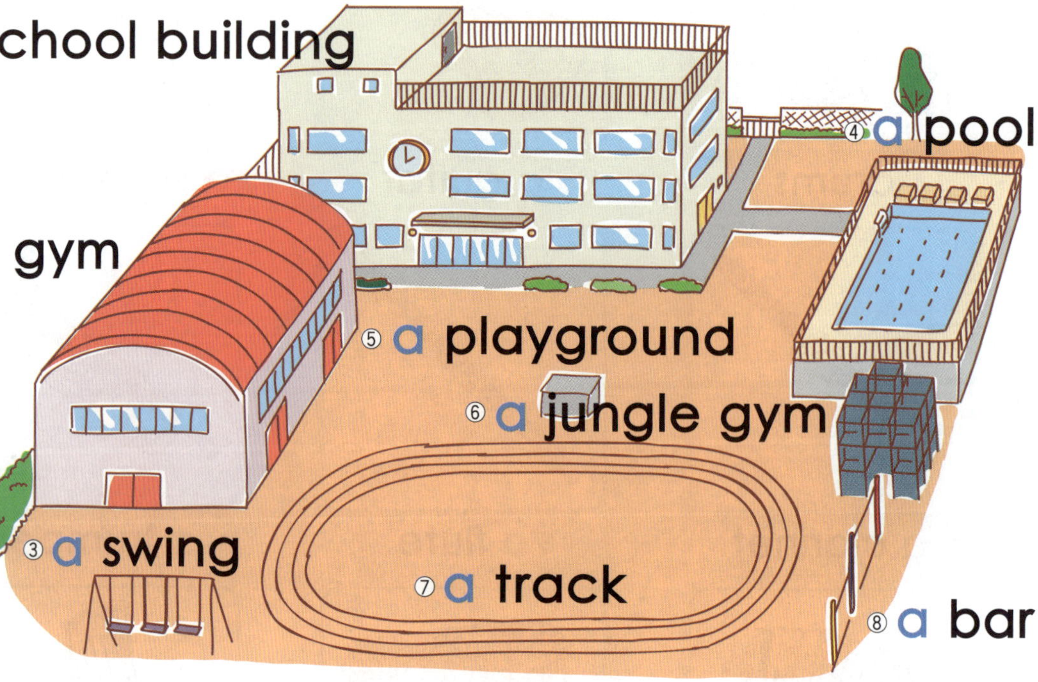


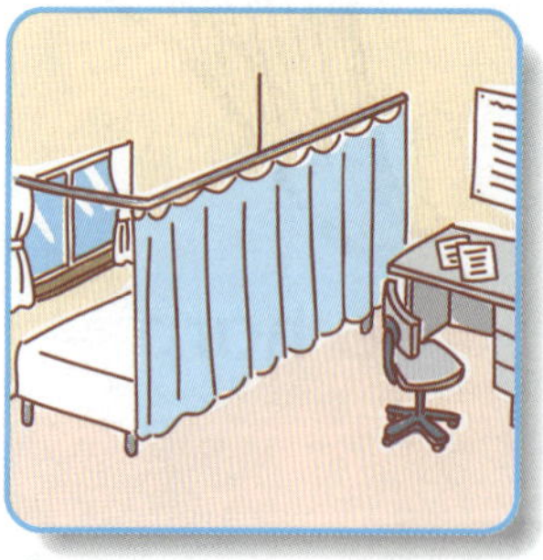

⑨ a nurse's room

⑩ a principal's room

⑪ a teachers' room

⑫ a computer room

⑬ a library

⑭
This is our elementary school.
We have a computer room.

⑮ Japanese

⑯ math

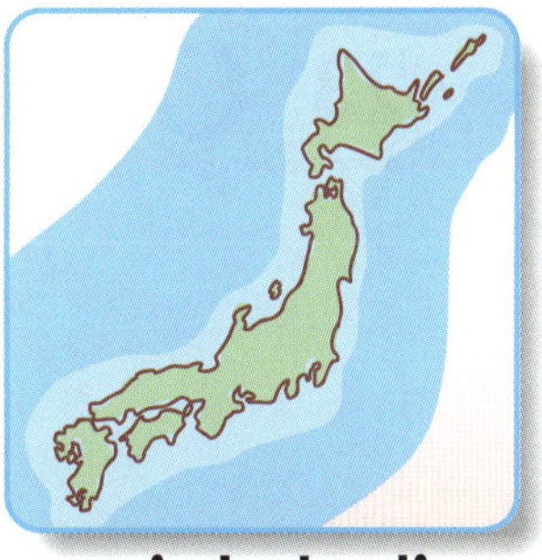

⑰ social studies

⑱ science

⑲ music

⑳ fine arts

㉑ PE

㉒ English

㉓
What's your favorite subject?

It's PE.

## LET'S TRY

すきな教科を線でむすびましょう。

1  •

2  •

• 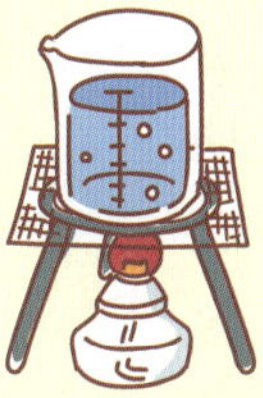

• 

• 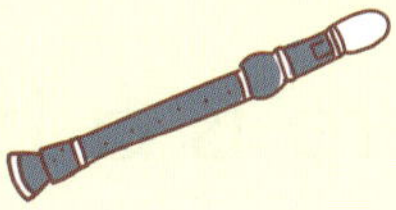

# Lesson 23 Our classroom わたしたちの教室(きょうしつ)

⑳ There is a blackboard in our classroom.

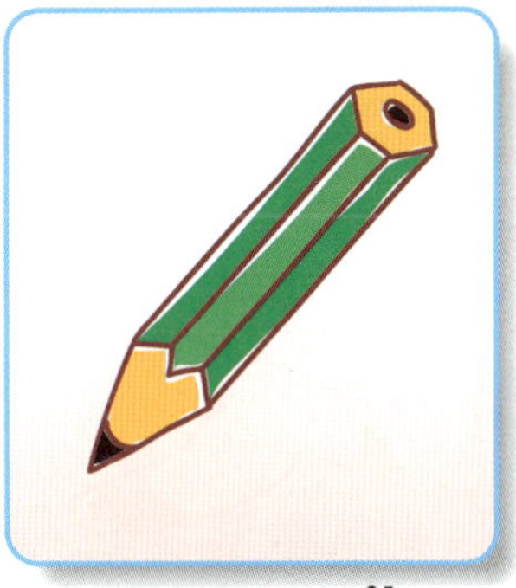

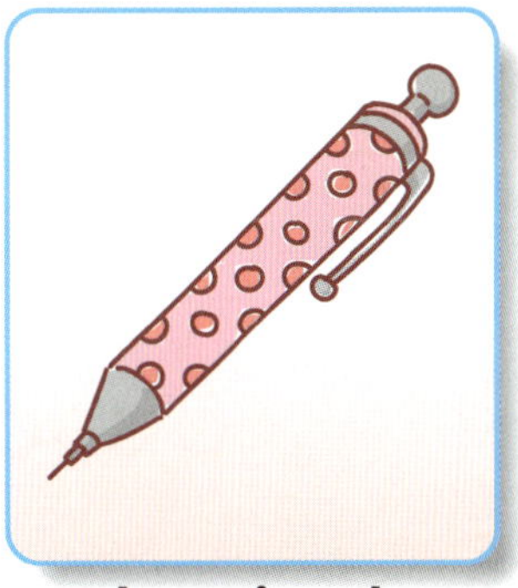

⑩ a pencil ⑪ a mechanical pencil ⑫ a pen

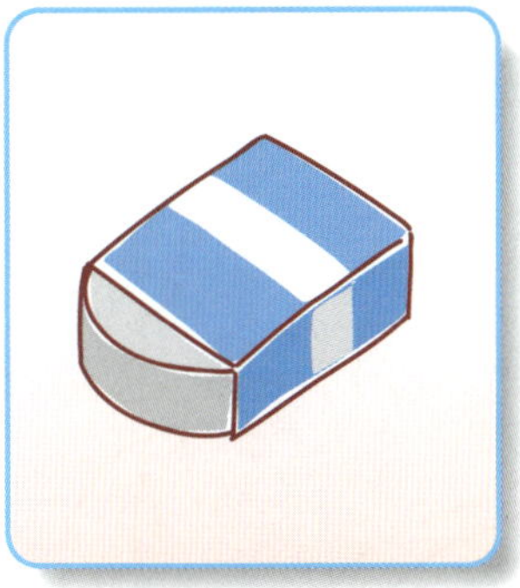

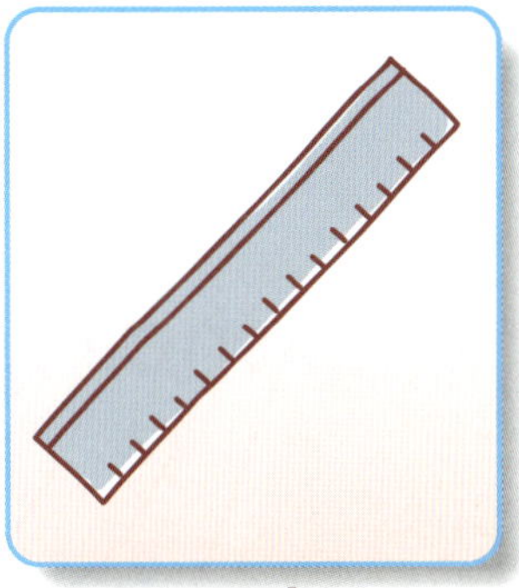

⑬ an eraser ⑭ a ruler ⑮ scissors

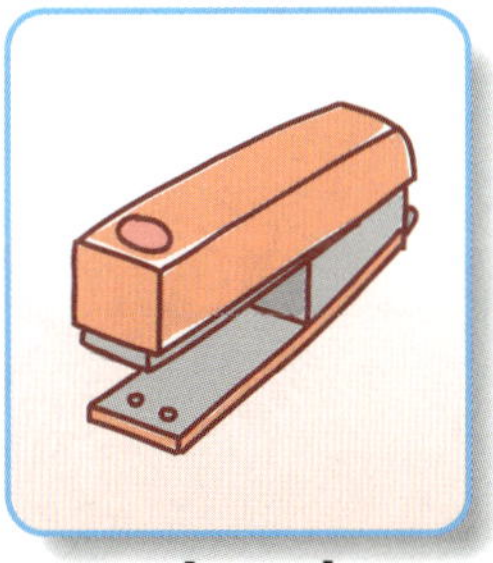

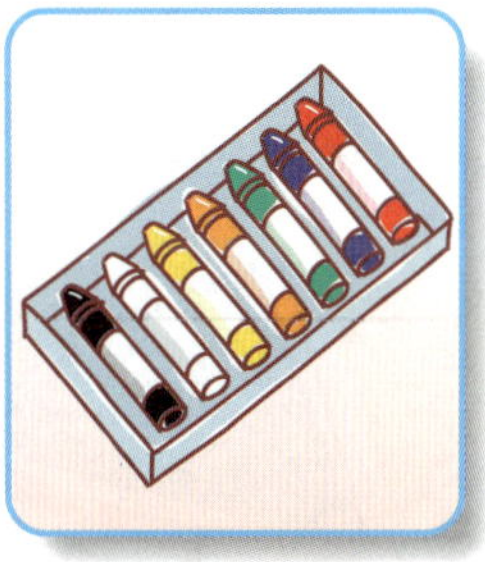

⑯ paste ⑰ a stapler ⑱ paint ⑲ crayons

㉑

There are many books on the desk.

## LET'S TRY

あうほうの絵をえらびましょう。

# Lesson 24 The sea 海(うみ)

㉓

Is there a lighthouse on the beach?

No, there isn't.

㉔
Are there any ships in the sea?

Yes. There are some ships.

## LET'S TRY

あう絵をえらびましょう。

# Lesson 25 Mountains 山（やま）

⑳

How many bears are there?

Two bears.

## LET'S TRY

あうほうの絵をえらびましょう。

# Lesson 26 At the zoo 動物園(どうぶつえん)

① a giraffe ② a zebra ③ an ostrich

④ an elephant

⑤ a lion

⑥ a cheetah

⑦ a gorilla

⑧ a chimpanzee

⑨ an alligator

⑩ a hippopotamus

⑪ a rhinoceros ⑫ a camel

㉑
Gorillas are big.
Chimpanzees are small.

⑬ a panda ⑭ a tiger

⑲ a penguin

⑳ a sea lion

⑮ a flamingo ⑯ a peacock

⑰ a koala ⑱ a kangaroo

㉒

A flamingo has long legs.
A penguin has short legs.

## LET'S TRY

すきな食べ物を線でむすびましょう。

# Lesson 27 On the farm 農場(のうじょう)

㉒

What animal do you have?

I have a rabbit.

## LET'S TRY

あう絵をえらびましょう。

# Lesson 28 Time and the days of the week 時間と曜日

⑱ What time is it now?

It's two thirty.

⑲ morning ⑳ afternoon ㉑ night

㉒ noon ㉓ midnight

㉔
Sunday
Monday
Tuesday
Wednesday
Thursday
Friday
Saturday

㉕ What day is it today?

It's Friday.

## LET'S TRY

あう絵をえらびましょう。

# Lesson 29 Seasons 季節（きせつ）

① spring

② March

③ April

④ May

⑤ summer

⑥ June

⑦ July

⑧ August

⑰

What season do you like best?

I like summer best.

## ⑨ fall

⑩ September

⑪ October

⑫ November

## ⑬ winter

⑭ December

⑮ January

⑯ February

⑱ When is your birthday?

It's in July.

## LET'S TRY

あう写真をえらびましょう。

# Lesson 30 Flowers and Trees 花と木

① cherry blossoms

② a pansy

③ a tulip

④ a dandelion

⑤ an azalea

⑥ a violet

⑦ a carnation

⑧ a lily

⑨ a rose

⑱

Which do you like better, tulips or roses?

I like roses better.

⑩ a hydrangea

⑪ a morning glory

⑫ a sunflower

⑬ a cactus

⑭ a cosmos

⑮ a dahlia

⑯ a pine tree

⑰ a bamboo

⑲ What color is the flower?

It's yellow.

## LET'S TRY

あう絵をえらびましょう。

# Lesson 31 Vehicles 乗り物

① a train

② a subway

③ a bus

④ a taxi

⑤ a monorail

⑥ a tricycle

⑦ a bicycle

⑧ a motorcycle

⑨ a balloon

⑩ a helicopter

⑪ an airplane

⑲

My mother goes to work by train.

⑫ an ambulance

⑬ a police car

⑯ a garbage truck

⑭ a truck

⑮ a fire engine

⑱ a crane truck

⑰ a bulldozer

⑳ How do you go to school?

By bus.

## LET'S TRY

あう絵をえらびましょう。

# Lesson 32 Jobs 仕事

① a baseball player

② an actor

③ a singer

④ a pilot

⑤ a flight attendant

⑥ an astronaut

⑦ a cartoonist

⑧ a painter

⑨ a writer

⑩ a carpenter

⑪ a cook

⑫ a farmer

㉒

My father is a doctor.

My mother is an office worker.

⑬ a doctor

⑭ a nurse

⑮ a scientist

⑯ a fire fighter

⑰ a police officer

⑱ a teacher

⑲ a lawyer

⑳ a politician

㉑ an office worker

㉓
What do you want to be?

I want to be a baseball player.

## LET'S TRY

あう絵をえらびましょう。

# Lesson 33 Space うちゅう

⑲
Are you interested in the moon?

Yes, very much.

⑳ Are you interested in aliens?

Yes, a little.

## LET'S TRY

あう絵をえらびましょう。

# Lesson 34 High and low

高いと低い

① high　low

② heavy　light

③ thick　thin

④ deep　shallow

⑤ right　left

⑥ dark　light

⑬ This mountain is low.
That mountain is high.

⑦ hard　soft

⑧ clean　dirty

⑨ cold　hot

⑩ new　old

⑪ fast　slow

⑫ good　bad

## LET'S TRY

あう絵をえらびましょう。

# Lesson 35 My day

## 1日の生活

① get up

② wash my face

③ comb my hair

④ put on my clothes

⑤ eat breakfast

⑥ brush my teeth

⑦ leave home

⑧ get to school

⑨ listen to the teacher

⑩ raise my hand

⑪ eat lunch

⑫ talk with my friend

㉒ I get up at 7.

⑬ clean our classroom

⑭ return home

⑮ watch TV

⑯ play a video game

⑰ eat dinner

⑱ help my mother

⑲ do my homework

⑳ take a bath

㉑ go to bed

㉓ What time do you eat dinner?

At 6.

## LET'S TRY

あう絵をえらびましょう。

# この本にでてくる 英語の意味


## A

a 1つの 17
accordion アコーディオン 45
actor はいゆう，じょゆう 66
afternoon 午後 59
air conditioner エアコン 28
airplane 飛行機 64
album アルバム 33
alien エイリアン 68
alligator わに 54
alphabet アルファベット 4
am（わたしは）～です 18
ambulance 救急車 65
amusement park 遊園地 35
an 1つの 34
and ～と，そして 8
animal 動物 56
ankle 足首 13
any いくらか 51
apple りんご 38
apple pie アップルパイ 8
April 4月 60
apron エプロン 14
are（あなたは，あなたたちは，かれらは）～です 18
arm うで 13
asparagus アスパラガス 40
astronaut 宇宙飛行士 66
at ①（場所をしめして）～で 54
②（時間をしめして）～に 72
August 8月 60
aunt おば 23
Australia オーストラリア 20
azalea つつじ 62

## B

back 背中 13
backpack リュックサック 52
bad 悪い 71
badminton バドミントン 42
bag かばん 32
ball ボール 17
balloon 気球 64
ball park 野球場 35
bamboo 竹 63
banana バナナ 38
bank 銀行 36
bar てつぼう 46
barbecue バーベキュー 52
baseball 野球 42
baseball player 野球選手 66
basketball バスケットボール 42
bass ベース 44
bat バット 33
bath 入浴 73
bathroom ふろ 26
be am，is，are が to に続くときの形 67
beach 海岸 50
beach umbrella ビーチパラソル 50
beans 豆 41
bear くま 52
bed ベッド 32
bedroom しんしつ 26
bee はち 56
beef 牛肉 7
belt ベルト 15
best いちばん 60
better もっと 62
bicycle 自転車 64
big 大きい 54
birthday たん生日 61
black 黒，黒の 10
blackboard 黒板 48
blue 青，青の 10
blueberry ブルーベリー 38
boat ボート 51
body 体 12
book 本 33
bookcase 本箱 32
bookstore 書店 36
bowling ボーリング 43
boxing ボクシング 43
Brazil ブラジル 21
bread パン 6
breakfast 朝食 72
bridge 橋 52
broccoli ブロッコリー 40
brother 兄，弟 22
brown 茶色，茶色の 10
brush ブラシでみがく 72
bulldozer ブルドーザー 65
bus バス 64
bush やぶ 34
bus stop バス停 37
but しかし，でも 43
butter バター 6
butterfly ちょう 56
by（手段をしめして）～で 64

## C

cabbage キャベツ 40
cactus サボテン 63
cake ケーキ 8
calendar カレンダー 33
call 電話をする 17
camel らくだ 54
camera カメラ 32
Canada カナダ 21
candy あめ 8
cap ぼうし 15
car 車 24
cardigan カーディガン 14
carnation カーネーション 62
carpenter 大工 66
carrot にんじん 40
cartoonist まんが家 66
castanets カスタネット 44
cat ねこ 56
catch 受ける，受けとる 17
CD シーディー 32
CD player シーディープレイヤー 32
celery セロリ 40
cello チェロ 44
cell phone けいたい電話 29
chair いす 33
chalk チョーク 48
cheek ほお 12
cheese チーズ 6
cheetah チーター 54
cherry さくらんぼ 38
cherry blossoms さくら 62
chest 胸 13
chestnut くり 39
chicken 鳥肉 7
chimney えんとつ 24
chimpanzee チンパンジー 54
chin あご 12
China 中国 20
chipmunk りす 52
chocolate チョコレート 8
cicada せみ 53
circle 円 11
clap 手をたたく，はくしゅをする 16
clarinet クラリネット 45
classroom 教室 48
class schedule 時間割 48
clean ①きれいな 71
②そうじをする 73
clock 時計 48
clothing 衣類 14

cloud 雲 69
cocoa ココア 9
coconut ココナッツ 39
coffee コーヒー 9
cola コーラ 9
cold 冷たい 71
color 色 10
comb (かみを)とかす 72
comic book まんがの本 33
computer コンピューター 29
computer room コンピュータールーム 46
convenience store コンビニエンスストアー 37
cook ①料理をする 17
②コック 66
cookie クッキー 8
corn とうもろこし 40
cosmos コスモス 63
country こうがい，いなか 34
cousin いとこ 23
cow 牛 57
crab かに 50
crane truck クレーン車 65
crayons クレヨン 49
cream puff シュークリーム 8
crosswalk 横断歩道 37
crow からす 56
cucumber きゅうり 40
cup カップ 30
cupboard たな 31
curry and rice カレーライス 7
curtain カーテン 32
cushion クッション 29
cymbals シンバル 44

## D

dahlia ダリア 63
dance おどる 17
dandelion たんぽぽ 62
dark 暗い 70
daughter むすめ 23
day 日，1日 59
December 12月 61
deep 深い 70
deer しか 53
Denmark デンマーク 20
department store デパート 36
desk 机 33
dessert デザート 8
diamond ダイヤ，ひし形 11
dictionary 辞書 48
dining room ダイニング 26
dinner 夕食 73
dirty きたない 71
dish 大きい皿 31
do ①(「～しません」と説明する文を作る) 39
②(「～しますか」としつもんする文やその答えの文を作る) 40
③する 73
doctor 医者 67
does ①(「かれ(かのじょ)は～しません」とせつめいする文を作る) 43
②(「かれ(かのじょ)は～しますか」としつもんする文やその答えの文を作る) 44
doesn't does not を短くした形 45
dog 犬 56
dolphin いるか 51
don't do not を短くした形 41
donut ドーナツ 8
door ドア 17
down → sit 16
dragonfly とんぼ 53
drink 飲み物 8
drums ドラム 45
duck かも，あひる 57

## E

ear 耳 12
Earth 地球 69
eat 食べる 72
eggplant なす 41
Egypt エジプト 20
eight 8，8つの 19
eighteen 18 58
eighty 80 58
elbow ひじ 13
elementary school 小学校 46
elephant ぞう 54
eleven 11，11この 19
English 英語 47
entrance げんかん 26
eraser 消しゴム 49
expressway 高速道路 34
eye 目 12
eyebrow まゆげ 12
eyelash まつげ 12

## F

face 顔 12
factory 工場 37
fall 秋 61
family 家族 22
family restaurant ファミリーレストラン 37
farm 農場 56
farmer 農業をする人 66
fast 速い 71
father (dad) 父 22
favorite 大好きな 34
February 2月 61
fence フェンス 25
fifteen 15 58
fifty 50 58
fig いちじく 39
fine arts 図画工作 47
finger 指 13
fire 火 52
fire engine 消ぼう車 65
fire fighter 消ぼう士 67
fire station 消ぼうしょ 37
fish 魚 7
five 5，5つの 18
flamingo フラミンゴ 55
flight attendant スチュワード，スチュワーデス 66
floor ゆか 29
flower 花 63
flower bed 花だん 25
flute フルート 45
fly 飛ぶ 17
food 食べ物 6
foot 足 13
fork フォーク 31
forty 40 58
four 4，4つの 18
fourteen 14 58
fox きつね 53
France フランス 20
French fries フライドポテト 6
Friday 金曜日 59
friend 友達 72
frog かえる 57
from (場所をしめして)～出身で，～から 21
front 正面 in *front* of ～の正面に 36
fruit くだもの 38
frying pan フライパン 30

## G

garage ガレージ 24
garbage truck せいそう車 65
garden 庭 25
garlic にんにく 41

**gas stove** ガスコンロ 31
**gate** 門 24
**Germany** ドイツ 20
**get** ①*get* up 起きる 72
②*get* to 着く 72
**ginger** しょうが 41
**giraffe** きりん 54
**glass** グラス 31
**glasses** めがね 15
**globe** 地球ぎ 32
**glove** グローブ 32
**gloves** 手ぶくろ 15
**go** ①行く 35
②*go* to bed ねる 73
**goat** やぎ 57
**goggles** ゴーグル 50
**golf** ゴルフ 43
**good** よい 71
**gorilla** ゴリラ 54
**grandfather(grandpa)** 祖父 22
**grandmother(grandma)** 祖母 22
**grapefruit** グレープフルーツ 38
**grapes** ぶどう 38
**gray** ねずみ色，ねずみ色の 10
**Great Britain** イギリス 20
**green** 緑，緑の 10
**green pepper** ピーマン 40
**green tea** 緑茶 9
**guitar** ギター 45
**gum** ガム 8
**gym** 体育館 46
**gymnastics** 器械体そう 42

## H

**hair** かみの毛 12
**hair dryer** ドライヤー 27
**ham and eggs** ハムエッグ 6
**hamburger** ハンバーガー 6
**hand** 手 13
**handkerchief** ハンカチ 15
**hard** 固い 71
**harmonica** ハーモニカ 44
**harp** ハープ 45
**has**（かれは，かのじょは）もっている 55
**hat** ぼうし 15
**have** もっている 46
**he** かれは 43
**head** 頭 13
**heart** ハート形 11
**heavy** 重い 70
**heel** かかと 13
**helicopter** ヘリコプター 64
**help** てつだう 73
**hen** めんどり 56
**high** 高い 70
**high jump** 高とび 42
**hill** おか 35
**hip** こし 13
**hippopotamus** かば 54
**home** ①家 72
②家へ 72
**homework** 宿題 73
**horse** 馬 57
**hospital** 病院 36
**hot** 熱い 71
**hot dog** ホットドッグ 6
**hotel** ホテル 35
**house** 家 24
**how** ①*How* old…? どのくらい年をとった，いくつの 18
②どのように *How* do you go to school? あなたはどのように学校へ行きますか。 65
**hundred** 100 58
**husband** 夫 23
**hydrangea** あじさい 63

## I

**I** わたしは 18
**ice cream** アイスクリーム 9
**I'm** I am を短くした形 21
**in** ①（場所をしめして）～の中に 26
②（月，季節などをしめして）～に 61
**India** インド 20
**inner tube** うきわ 50
**instrument** 楽器 44
**intercom** インターフォン 24
**interested** be *interested* in ～にきょうみをもっている 68
**intersection** 交差点 37
**is** ～です 21
**island** 島 51
**isn't** is not を短くした形 30
**it** ①それは 23
②（時こく，日などをさす） 58
**Italy** イタリア 20
**it's** it is を短くした形 28

## J

**jacket** ジャケット 14
**jam** ジャム 6
**January** 1月 61
**Japan** 日本 20
**Japanese**（じゅぎょうの）国語 47
**jeans** ジーンズ 14
**job** 仕事 66
**juice** ジュース 9
**July** 7月 60
**jump** ジャンプする 16
**June** 6月 60
**jungle gym** ジャングルジム 46

## K

**kangaroo** カンガルー 55
**kettle** やかん 30
**keyboard** キーボード 29
**kitchen** キッチン 26
**kiwi** キウイ 39
**knee** ひざ 13
**knife** ナイフ 31
**koala** コアラ 55
**Korea** 韓国（かんこく） 20

## L

**lake** 湖 35
**lawn** しばふ 25
**lawyer** べんご士 67
**leave** 出発する 72
**leek** ねぎ 41
**left** 左の 70
**leg** 足 13
**lemon** レモン 38
**let's**（さそいかけるときに）～しましょう。 35
**lettuce** レタス 40
**library** 図書室 46
**light** ①ライト 28
②軽い 70
③明るい 70
**lighthouse** 灯台 51
**like** 好きだ 38
**lily** ゆり 62
**lion** ライオン 54
**lip** くちびる 12
**listen** *listen* to ～を聞く 72
**little** a *little* 少しは 69
**living room** 居間（いま） 26
**long** 長い 55
**low** 低い 70
**lunch** 昼食 72

## M

**magazine** ざっし 28
**mango** マンゴー 39

**many** たくさんの 49
**map** 地図 48
**marathon** マラソン 42
**March** 3月 60
**math** 算数，数学 47
**May** 5月 60
**mechanical pencil** シャープペンシル 49
**melon** メロン 38
**microwave oven** 電子レンジ 30
**midnight** 真夜中 59
**milk** 牛にゅう 9
**Milky Way** 天の川 68
**mine** わたしのもの 31
**mirror** かがみ 27
**mole** もぐら 56
**Monday** 月曜日 59
**monkey** さる 52
**monorail** モノレール 64
**moon** 月 68
**morning** 朝 59
**morning glory** あさがお 63
**mother(mom)** 母 22
**motorcycle** オートバイ 64
**mountain** 山 52
**mouse** ねずみ 57
**mouth** 口 12
**much** たくさんの very much とても 68
**museum** 博物館，美じゅつ館 36
**mushroom** マッシュルーム 41
**music** 音楽 47
**my** わたしの 12

## N

**name** 名前 21
**nameplate** 表札 24
**neck** 首 13
**new** 新しい 71
**newspaper** 新聞 28
**next** となりに *next* to ～のとなりに 36
**night** 夜 59
**nine** 9，9つの 19
**nineteen** 19 58
**ninety** 90 58
**No** いいえ 27
**noon** 正午 59
**Norway** ノルウェー 20
**nose** 鼻 12
**not** ～でない，～しない 27
**notebook** ノート 48
**November** 11月 61
**now** 今 58
**number** 数 18
**nurse** かんごし 67
**nurse's room** ほけん室 46

## O

**October** 10月 61
**octopus** たこ 51
**of** （部分をしめして）～の 36
**office worker** 事む所で働く人 67
**often** しばしば 42
**oil** 油 30
**okra** オクラ 41
**old** ①年をとった 18
②古い 71
**on**（場所をしめして）～の上に，～に 33
**one** 1，1つの 18
**onion** たまねぎ 40
**open** 開ける 17
**or** それとも 62
**orange** ①オレンジ色，オレンジ色の 10
②オレンジ 38
**orchard** 果じゅ園 34
**ostrich** だちょう 54
**our** わたしたちの 24
**owl** ふくろう 53

## P

**paint** 絵の具 49
**painter** 画家 66
**pajamas** パジャマ 14
**palm tree** ココヤシ 51
**panda** パンダ 55
**pansy** パンジー 62
**pants** ズボン 14
**parents** 両親 22
**park** 公園 37
**parking lot** ちゅう車場 37
**parsley** パセリ 41
**pasta** パスタ 7
**paste** のり 49
**PE** 体育 47
**peach** もも 38
**peacock** くじゃく 55
**pear** なし 39
**pen** ペン 49
**pencil** えんぴつ 49
**penguin** ペンギン 55
**pentagon** 五角形 11
**pepper** こしょう 30
**persimmon** かき 39
**photo** 写真 29
**piano** ピアノ 44
**picture** 絵 29
**pig** ぶた 56
**pigeon** はと 56
**pillow** まくら 32
**pilot** パイロット 66
**pineapple** パイナップル 39
**pine tree** 松 63
**pink** ピンク，ピンクの 10
**pizza** ピザ 6
**place** 場所 34
**plate** 取り皿 31
**play**（遊び，スポーツ，楽器のえんそうなどを）する 42
**playground** 運動場 46
**please**（人に何かをたのむときに）どうぞ 16
**police car** パトロールカー 65
**police officer** けいさつ官 67
**police station** けいさつしょ 37
**politician** 政治家 67
**pond** 池 25
**pool** プール 46
**popcorn** ポップコーン 8
**pork** ぶた肉 7
**poster** ポスター 33
**post office** ゆう便局 37
**pot** 深なべ 30
**potato** じゃがいも 40
**potato chips** ポテトチップス 8
**principal's room** 校長室 46
**printer** プリンター 29
**pudding** プリン 8
**pumpkin** かぼちゃ 41
**purple** むらさき，むらさきの 10
**put** *put* on（服を）着る 72

## R

**rabbit** うさぎ 56
**radish** ラディッシュ 41
**rain** 雨 69
**rain boots** 長ぐつ 15
**rainbow** にじ 69
**raincoat** レインコート 14
**raise** もち上げる *raise* a hand 手をあげる 72
**recorder** リコーダー 44
**rectangle** 長方形 11
**red** 赤，赤の 10
**refrigerator** 冷ぞう庫 31
**remote control** リモコン 28
**return** もどる 73

rhinoceros さい 54
rice ごはん 7
rice field 田 34
right 右の 70
ring ①輪 11
②指輪 15
rinse リンス 27
river 川 52
road 道 35
rocket ロケット 68
roof 屋根 24
room 部屋 32
rose バラ 62
rug じゅうたん 28
rugby ラグビー 42
ruler じょうぎ 49
run 走る 16
Russia ロシア 20

## S

salad サラダ 7
salt 塩 30
sandwich サンドイッチ 6
satellite 人工えい星 68
Saturday 土曜日 59
sausage ソーセージ 6
saxophone サックス 45
scale 体重計 27
scarf マフラー 15
school 学校 37
school building 校しゃ 46
science 理科 47
scientist 科学者 67
scissors はさみ 49
sea 海 51
seagull かもめ 50
sea lion あしか 55
season 季節 60
September 9月 61
seven 7、7つの 19
seventeen 17 58
seventy 70 58
shake シェーク 9
shallow 浅い 70
shampoo シャンプー 27
shape 形 10
shark さめ 51
she かのじょは 42
sheep 羊 57
shell 貝 50
sherbet シャーベット 9
ship 船 51
shirt シャツ 14
shoes くつ 15
shooting star 流れ星 68
short 短い 55
shoulder 肩 13
shower シャワー 27
shrimp えび 51
shut 閉める 17
shutter シャッター 24
sing 歌う 17
Singapore シンガポール 20
singer 歌手 66
sink 流し 30
sister 姉，妹 22
sit すわる *sit* down すわる 16
six 6、6つの 18
sixteen 16 58
sixty 60 58
skateboarding スケートボード 43
skating スケート 43
skiing スキー 43
skip スキップする 16
skirt スカート 14
skunk スカンク 53
sky 空 34
slippers スリッパ 27
slow おそい 71
small 小さい 54
snake へび 53
snow 雪 69
soap せっけん 27
soccer サッカー 42
social studies (じゅぎょうの) 社会 47
socks くつ下 15
sofa ソファー 28
soft やわらかい 71
softball ソフトボール 42
soft ice cream ソフトクリーム 9
some いくつかの 51
son むすこ 23
song 歌 5
soup スープ 6
space 宇宙 68
space shuttle スペースシャトル 68
Spain スペイン 20
sparrow すずめ 56
speaker スピーカー 48
spider くも 53
spinach ほうれん草 41
spoon スプーン 31
sport スポーツ 42
spring 春 60
square 四角形 11
squid いか 51
stairs 階だん 26
stand 立つ *stand* up 立ち上がる 16
stapler ホッチキス 49
star ①星形 11
②星 68
station 駅 36
steak ステーキ 7
step ふみだん 24
stereo ステレオ 29
stew シチュー 7
stomach おなか 13
stone 石 52
stop 止まる 16
strawberry いちご 38
street 通り 36
subject 教科 47
subway 地下鉄 64
sugar さとう 30
suit スーツ 14
summer 夏 60
sun 太陽 69
Sunday 日曜日 59
sunflower ひまわり 63
supermarket スーパーマーケット 36
surfing サーフィン 43
swallow つばめ 56
swan 白鳥 57
sweater セーター 14
sweatshirt トレーナー 14
swimming 水泳 43
swimsuit 水着 50
swing ブランコ 46
Switzerland スイス 20

## T

table テーブル 28
tablecloth テーブルクロス 30
table tennis たっきゅう 42
take *take* a bath ふろに入る 73
talk 話す 72
tambourine タンバリン 44
taxi タクシー 64
tea 紅茶 9
teacher 先生 67
teachers' room しょく員室 46
teapot きゅうす 30
teeth tooth(歯)の複数形 72
telephone 電話 28

**temple** 寺 34
**ten** 10，10この 19
**tennis** テニス 42
**tent** テント 52
**textbook** 教科書 48
**that** あれは，あれが 25
**the** ①(ただひとつしかないものにつける) *the* alphabet 4
②the その 32
③the(楽器，用具などにつける)play *the* piano 44
**theater** げきじょう 36
**then** それなら 33
**there** *there* is(are)… ～がある 48
**The United States** アメリカ 21
**they** それらは，かれらは 33
**thick** 厚い 70
**thin** うすい 70
**thirteen** 13 58
**thirty** 30 58
**this** これは，これが 22
**three** 3，3つの 18
**throw** 投げる 17
**thumb** 親指 13
**thunder** かみなり 69
**Thursday** 木曜日 59
**tie** ネクタイ 15
**tiger** とら 55
**time** 時間 58
**tissue** ティッシュ 27
**to**(行き先をしめして)～へ 35
**today** 今日 59
**toe** 足の指 13
**toilet** トイレ 26
**tomato** トマト 40
**tongue** 舌(した) 12
**tooth** 歯 12
**toothbrush** 歯ブラシ 27
**touch** さわる 12
**town** 町 36
**track**(運動場の)トラック 46
**track and field** 陸上競技 42
**traffic light** 信号 36
**train** 電車 64
**trash can** ごみ箱 30
**tree** 木 62
**triangle** ①三角形 11
②トライアングル 44
**tricycle** 三輪車 64
**truck**(車の)トラック 65
**trumpet** トランペット 45
**T-shirt** ティーシャツ 14
**Tuesday** 火曜日 59
**tulip** チューリップ 62
**turn** 向きをかえる 16
**turnip** かぶ 41
**turtle** かめ 50
**TV**(**television**)テレビ 28
**twelve** 12 19
**twenty** 20 58
**twenty-one** 21 58
**two** 2，2つの 18

## U

**UFO** ユーフォー 68
**uncle** おじ 23
**under**(場所をしめして)～の下に 33
**uniform** ユニフォーム 14
**up** → stand 16

## V

**vacuum cleaner** そうじ機 29
**vase** 花びん 28
**vegetable** 野菜 40
**vehicle** 乗り物 64
**vending machine** 自動はん売機 37
**very** not …*very* あまり～でない 43
**vest** ベスト 14
**video game** テレビゲーム 73
**violet** すみれ 62
**violin** バイオリン 44
**volleyball** バレーボール 42

## W

**walk** 歩く 16
**wall** かべ 25
**walnut** くるみ 39
**want** *want* to … ～したい 67
**wash** 洗う 72
**washing machine** せんたく機 27
**watch** じっと見る 73
**water** 水 9
**watermelon** すいか 38
**wave** 波 50
**we** わたしたちは 46
**wedding dress** ウエディングドレス 14
**Wednesday** 水曜日 59
**week** 週 58
**weight lifting** ウエイトリフティング 43
**well** うまく 43
**whale** くじら 51
**what** ①何 28
②どんな 56
**what's** what is を短くした形 47
**when** いつ 61
**where** どこで，どこに 20
**which** どちらが 62
**white** 白，白の 10
**who** だれ 23
**whose** だれの 31
**wife** つま 23
**wind** 風 69
**window** まど 17
**winter** 冬 61
**with**(相手をしめして)～と 72
**woodpecker** きつつき 53
**woods** 森 34
**work** 仕事 64
**world** 世界 20
**wrist** 手首 13
**writer** 作家 66

## X

**xylophone** もっきん 45

## Y

**yacht** ヨット 51
**year** 年れい 18
**yellow** 黄色，黄色の 10
**Yes** はい 26
**yogurt** ヨーグルト 8
**you** あなたは 18
**your** あなたの，あなたたちの 12

## Z

**zebra** しまうま 54
**zoo** 動物園 54

飯塚佐一（イイヅカサイチ）
早稲田大学教育学部卒業後、海城中学校・高等学校にて英語教諭を務め、同校教頭、那須高原海城中学・高等学校校長を歴任。現在、日本英語表現学会理事を務める。これまで、文部科学省派遣アメリカ教育視察団に参加し、検定教科書、「フェイバリット英和辞典」などの辞書類、数多くの学習参考書などを執筆、幅広く英語教育に貢献している。

中村匡克（ナカムラマサカツ）
早稲田大学教育学部卒業後、同大学院を修了。元工学院大学教授、現在日本英語表現学会顧問、日本カレドニア学会理事。早稲田大学をはじめカルチャーセンターなどで講師を務める。シェイクスピアや聖書についての専門家でもある。これまで、「ブライト英和辞典」「ワードパル英和辞典」などの編集や、「英語教育のための文学案内辞典」など多くを執筆。

テリー オサダ
テキサス大学卒業後、シアトル大学大学院を修了。英語教育法を取得。「NHK英語で遊ぼう」を10年間担当し、「NHKトークアンドトーク」、「NHKビジネス英語」、「NHK基礎英語1・3」の講師を歴任。

New ABC of ENGLISH
単語編（新装改訂新版）

2004年2月1日 新装改訂新版第1刷発行
2024年2月3日 新装改訂新版第8刷発行

| | |
|---|---|
| 著者 | 飯塚 佐一 |
| 監修者 | 中村 匡克 |
| ネイティブ監修者 | テリー オサダ |
| 企画・制作 | カルチャーアイ |
| 編集 | アポロ企画 |
| 発行者 | 亀井 崇雄 |
| 発行所 | 創英社／三省堂書店<br>〒101-0051 東京都千代田区神田神保町1-1<br>TEL.03-3291-2295 |
| 印刷 | リーブルテック |

イラスト 河田 邦広　デザイン 西田 慧一

Printed in Japan　禁無断転載・複製　ISBN978-4-88142-104-8
*定価はカバーに表示してあります。
*乱丁・落丁はお取り替えいたします。

## 英語でいうと・・・

# ア

| | |
|---|---|
| アイスクリーム | ice cream |
| 青 | blue |
| 赤 | red |
| 明かり | light |
| 秋 | fall |
| 脚(あし) | leg |
| 足 | foot |
| 頭 | head |
| 油 | oil |
| あめ | candy |
| 雨 | rain |
| アルバム | album |
| 家 | house |
| 石 | stone |
| 医者 | doctor |
| いす | chair |
| いちご | strawberry |
| いとこ | cousin |
| 犬 | dog |
| 居間(いま) | living room |
| 妹 | sister |
| 衣類 | clothing |
| 色 | color |
| うさぎ | rabbit |
| 牛 | cow |
| うちゅう | space |
| うで | arm |
| 馬 | horse |
| 海 | sea |
| 絵 | picture |
| 英語 | English |
| 駅 | station |
| 絵の具 | paint |
| えんぴつ | pencil |
| お母さん | mother |
| おじいさん | grandfather |
| おじさん | uncle |
| お父さん | father |
| 弟 | brother |
| お兄さん | brother |
| お姉さん | sister |
| おばあさん | grandmother |
| おばさん | aunt |
| オレンジ | orange |
| 音楽 | music |

# カ

| | |
|---|---|
| 顔 | face |
| 歌手 | singer |
| カスタネット | castanets |
| 風 | wind |
| 家族 | family |
| 学校 | school |
| カップ | cup |
| かばん | bag |
| かぼちゃ | pumpkin |
| かみの毛 | hair |
| ガム | gum |
| カメラ | camera |
| 体 | body |
| カレーライス | curry and rice |
| カレンダー | calendar |
| 川 | river |
| 木 | tree |
| 黄色 | yellow |
| 季節 | season |
| ギター | guitar |
| キッチン | kitchen |
| 牛肉 | beef |
| 牛にゅう | milk |
| 教科書 | textbook |
| 教室 | classroom |
| きりん | giraffe |
| 銀行 | bank |
| くだもの | fruit |
| 口 | mouth |
| くつ | shoes |
| クッキー | cookie |
| 首 | neck |
| くま | bear |
| 雲 | cloud |
| グラス | glass |
| 車 | car |
| 黒 | black |
| グローブ | glove |
| ケーキ | cake |
| 消しゴム | eraser |
| コアラ | koala |
| 公園 | park |
| 紅茶 | tea |
| コーヒー | coffee |
| 国語 | Japanese |
| 黒板 | blackboard |
| こしょう | pepper |
| ごはん | rice |
| コンピューター | computer |

# サ

| | |
|---|---|
| 魚 | fish |
| さくらんぼ | cherry |
| サッカー | soccer |
| ざっし | magazine |
| さとう | sugar |
| 皿 | plate, dish |
| サラダ | salad |
| さる | monkey |
| 算数，数学 | math |
| ジーンズ | jeans |
| シェーク | shake |
| 塩 | salt |
| 時間 | time |
| 時間割 | class schedule |
| 仕事 | job |
| 辞書 | dictionary |
| シチュー | stew |
| 自転車 | bicycle |
| しまうま | zebra |
| 社会 | social studies |
| じゃがいも | potato |
| 写真 | photo |
| ジャム | jam |
| シュークリーム | cream puff |
| ジュース | juice |
| 書店 | bookstore |
| 白 | white |
| 寝室(しんしつ) | bedroom |
| 新聞 | newspaper |
| 水泳 | swimming |
| すいか | watermelon |
| スーパーマーケット | supermarket |
| スカート | skirt |
| 図画工作 | fine arts |
| スキー | skiing |
| ステーキ | stake |
| スプーン | spoon |
| スポーツ | sport |
| ズボン | pants |
| セーター | sweater |
| せかい | world |
| せっけん | soap |
| 先生 | teacher |
| ぞう | elephant |

# New ABC of ENGLISH
# 指導用マニュアル

## 単語編

### ●授業で使う英語表現●

| | |
|---|---|
| Let's start our English lesson now. | さあ，授業を始めましょう。 |
| Are you ready? | 準備はいいですか。 |
| Listen to me carefully. | わたしのいうことを注意して聞きなさい。 |
| Open your textbooks to page 15. | 教科書の15ページを開きなさい。 |
| Repeat after me. | わたしのあとについていいなさい。 |
| Repeat after the CD. | ＣＤのあとについていいなさい。 |
| Read the text aloud. | 教科書を声に出して読みなさい。 |
| How do you say this in English?<br>What is the English for this? | これは英語で何といいますか。 |
| Try it again. | もう１度やりなさい。 |
| Say it louder, please. | もっと大きな声でいってください。 |
| I beg your pardon. | もう１度いってください。 |
| Next, please. | はい，次の人。／はい，次の問題。 |
| Good! | よくできました。 |
| Excellent! | 大変よくできました。 |
| That's all for today. | 今日の授業はこれまでです。 |

## Lesson 1　The alphabet アルファベット

**語句**

the（ただひとつしかないものにつける）*the* alphabet
alphabet アルファベット　song 歌

**留意点**

● アルファベットの発音を練習します。「エー，ビー，シー」などとならないように注意して指導してください。
● 外来語として使われていることばを中心に集めました。スペリングにふれる必要は特にありません。聞きとりと発音の練習をさせましょう。
● ここでは次の単語をあつかいます。
apple book cake dog egg fish glove hat iron jam king lemon monkey net OK piano queen racket spoon tiger uniform videotape window X-ray yellow zebra
● たとえばアルファベットのAの発音は[ei]ですが，appleのaの発音は[æ]です。このようにアルファベットの発音と，それが単語になったときの発音は，必ずしも同じではないことを，子ども達に気づかせるようにしましょう。

**LET'S SING**

The ABC Song

## Lesson 2　Food 食べ物

**語句**

food 食べ物　bread パン
butter バター　jam ジャム
hamburger ハンバーガー　hot dog ホットドッグ
French fries フライドポテト　sandwich サンドイッチ
pizza ピザ　ham and eggs ハムエッグ
cheese チーズ　sausage ソーセージ
soup スープ　steak ステーキ
pasta パスタ　curry and rice カレーライス
stew シチュー　salad サラダ
rice ごはん　beef 牛肉
pork ぶた肉　chicken 鳥肉
fish 魚

**留意点**

● 食べ物は誰でも興味や関心があるはずです。ましてや，日常的に身近に存在しますから，子ども達は覚えやすいでしょう。
● ham and eggs, curry and rice と and がついたものがあります。発音に注意してください。軽くアンとしか聞こえないでしょう。その発音どおりに覚えましょう。
● 日本語には多くの外来語があります。元の英語の発音と外来語は同じでないことに気づかせることが大切です。
● 次のことばはまちがえやすいので注意しましょう。
パン　bread
フライドポテト　French fries

**LET'S TRY**

外来語になっている食べ物の聞きとりの練習をします。
問題　1　omelet
　　　2　bacon and eggs
　　　3　hamburger steak
　　　4　toast

## Lesson 3　Dessert and Drink デザートと飲み物

**語句**

dessert デザート　and ～と，そして
drink 飲み物　candy あめ
chocolate チョコレート　gum ガム
potato chips ポテトチップス　popcorn ポップコーン
donut ドーナツ　apple pie アップルパイ
cake ケーキ　cream puff シュークリーム
cookie クッキー　pudding プリン
yogurt ヨーグルト　ice cream アイスクリーム
soft ice cream ソフトクリーム
sherbet シャーベット　cola コーラ
juice ジュース　shake シェーク
milk 牛乳　coffee コーヒー
tea 紅茶　cocoa ココア
green tea 緑茶　water 水

**留意点**

● dessert（デザート）のスペリングに注意しましょう。desert では砂漠です。
● 次のことばはまちがえやすいので注意しましょう。
シュークリーム　cream puff
プリン　pudding
ソフトクリーム　soft ice cream

**LET'S TRY**

外来語になっている食べ物の聞きとりの練習をします。
問題　1　orange juice
　　　2　marshmallow
　　　3　birthday cake
　　　4　vanilla ice cream

## Lesson 4　Colors and Shapes 色と形

**語句**

color 色　shape 形
white 白，白の　yellow 黄色，黄色の
orange オレンジ色，オレンジ色の
green 緑，緑の　purple 紫，紫の
pink ピンク，ピンクの　red 赤，赤の
brown 茶色，茶色の　gray ねずみ色，ねずみ色の
black 黒，黒の　blue 青，青の
star 星形　circle 円
triangle 三角形　square 四角形
rectangle 長方形　pentagon 五角形
ring 輪　heart ハート形
diamond ダイヤ，ひし形

**和訳**

yellow ring 黄色の輪
blue diamond 青いダイヤ

**留意点**

● ここで習う色を表すことばは，名詞としても形容詞としても使われます。
例　Red is a sign of danger.（赤は危険のサインです。）
　　She has a red bicycle.
　　（彼女は赤い自転車をもっています。）
● 色を表すことばと，形を表すことばを別々に練習したあとは，orange star, pink circle のように色と形を組み合わせて練習します。p.11のイラストに色をぬらせましょう。

**LET'S TRY**

問題　1　blue star　2　purple circle
　　　3　orange triangle　4　white heart

## Lesson 5　My face and body わたしの顔と体

**語句**

my わたしの　face 顔
body 体　eyebrow まゆげ

hair かみの毛　　ear 耳
nose 鼻　　mouth 口
chin あご　　cheek ほお
eye 目　　eyelash まつげ
lip くちびる　　tongue 舌
tooth 歯　　head 頭
neck 首　　chest 胸
knee ひざ　　heel かかと
toe 足の指　　ankle 足首
stomach 腹　　elbow ひじ
wrist 手首　　finger 指
thumb 親指　　arm うで
hand 手　　hip 腰
foot 足　　leg 脚
back 背中　　shoulder 肩
touch さわる　　your あなたの，あなたたちの

**和訳**

Touch your ear, Ken. あなたの耳にさわってください，健。

**留意点**

- 手の指は，親指を thumb，人差し指から小指までを finger といいます。足の指は toe です。つま先は tiptoe といいます。
- hip は体の左右の張り出した腰骨のあたりを指します。尻は buttock です。
- 目，耳，ほお，くちびる，肩など２つあるものは，ふつう複数形で使います。
  例　Her eyes are blue.
  （彼女の目は青い色をしています。）
  A rabbit has long ears.
  （うさぎは長い耳をもっています。）
- tooth（歯）の複数形は teeth です。
- hair（かみの毛），eyelash（まつげ）は，１本１本を表すこともありますが，全体を表すこともあります。
  例　There was a hair in the soup.
  （スープの中にかみの毛が１本入っていました。）
  She has brown hair.　（彼女のかみの毛は茶色です。）
- Touch your ear, Ken. を使って練習しましょう。ただし，複数の相手に呼びかけるときは，名詞を複数形にします。
  例　Touch your noses.
  （鼻にさわってください。）
  Touch your heads.
  （頭にさわってください。）

**LET'S TRY**

問題　1　Touch your nose and eye.
　　　2　Touch your head and chest.

## Lesson 6　Clothing 身につけるもの

**語句**

clothing 衣類　　shirt シャツ
T-shirt ティーシャツ　　sweatshirt トレーナー
jacket ジャケット　　sweater セーター
vest ベスト　　cardigan カーディガン
suit スーツ　　jeans ジーンズ
pants ズボン　　skirt スカート
wedding dress ウエディングドレス
apron エプロン　　pajamas パジャマ
raincoat レインコート　　uniform ユニフォーム
cap ぼうし　　hat ぼうし
gloves 手ぶくろ　　scarf マフラー
belt ベルト　　tie ネクタイ
ring 指輪　　glasses めがね
handkerchief ハンカチ　　socks くつ下
shoes くつ　　rain boots 長ぐつ

**和訳**

Touch your pink T-shirt, Rika. あなたのピンク色のＴシャツにさわってください，里香。

**留意点**

- 次のことばはまちがえやすいので注意しましょう。
  トレーナー　sweatshirt
  マフラー　scarf
- 「ワイシャツ」は white shirt からきた外来語です。英語ではありません。
- ２つの部分からできあがっている jeans，pants，pajamas，gloves，glasses，socks，shoes，rain boots は常に複数形で使われます。数えるときは，a pair of ～，two pairs of ～といいます。
- Touch your ～. の文を使って練習しましょう。

**LET'S TRY**

問題　1　blue T-shirt
　　　2　white hat
　　　3　red shoes
　　　4　yellow handkerchief

## Lesson 7　Stand up, please. 立ってください。

**語句**

walk 歩く　　run 走る
jump ジャンプする　　skip スキップする
turn 向きをかえる　　stop 止まる
stand 立つ *stand* up 立ち上がる
sit すわる *sit* down すわる
clap 手をたたく，はくしゅをする
open 開ける　　a １つの
window 窓　　shut 閉める
door ドア　　cook 料理をする
catch 受ける，受けとる　　ball ボール
throw 投げる　　call 電話をする
sing 歌う　　dance おどる
fly 飛ぶ
please（人に何かをたのむときに）どうぞ

**和訳**

Stand up, please. 立ってください。

**留意点**

- 「～しなさい」と命令するときは，Stand up. のように，主語の you を省略し，動詞の原形で文を始めます。このような文を命令文といいます。命令文は強い口調でいうと命令のニュアンスになります。また，ふつうの口調で please をつけていうと，ていねいな表現となり，依頼のニュアンスになります。
  例　Stand up.
  （立ちなさい。）
  Stand up, please.
  （どうぞ立ってください。）
- 実際に命令しあって練習しましょう。その際，window，door，ball は特定のものになるので，a を the にします。
  例　Open the window, please.
  （窓を開けてください。）
  Throw the ball, please.
  （ボールを投げてください。）

**LET'S TRY**

問題　1　Sit down, please.
　　　2　Open the door, please.
　　　3　Stop, please.

## Lesson 8 Numbers 数

**語句**

number 数 one 1，1つの
two 2，2つの three 3，3つの
four 4，4つの five 5，5つの
six 6，6つの seven 7，7つの
eight 8，8つの nine 9，9つの
ten 10，10個の eleven 11，11個の
twelve 12，12個の
how *How* old …? どのくらい年をとった，いくつの
old 古い，年をとった
are（あなたは，あなたたちは，彼らは）〜です
you あなたは I わたしは
am（わたしは）〜です year 年れい

**和訳**

How old are you? あなたは何才ですか。/ I am eight years old. わたしは8才です。

**留意点**

● 1〜12の数字を覚えます。スペリングにはふれずに，暗記させます。そのあと，イラストの衣類の数と英語を関連づけるのがよいでしょう。

● 2つ以上のものを表す場合には，名詞の語尾に -s または -es をつけて複数形にします。
CDでは，sweater one sweater vests two vestsのように読みあげられます。CDのあとに続けて練習させましょう。

● 「1つのもの」を表すときに，特に「1つ」を強調したい場合には，名詞の前にoneをつけます。また，「1つ」を強調しない場合でも「1つ」の意味をもつaまたはanを名詞の前につけます。
例 I have one sweater.
I have a sweater.

● 「何才ですか」と年令をたずねるときは，How old〜? を使います。
例 How old are you? （あなたは何才ですか。）

● 「わたしは〜です」というときは，I am〜. を使います。
例 I am five years old. （わたしは5才です。）

**LET'S TRY**

問題 1 I'm seven years old.
2 I'm twelve years old.
3 I'm three years old.

## Lesson 9 The world 世界

**語句**

world 世界 Norway ノルウェー
Denmark デンマーク Great Britain イギリス
Spain スペイン France フランス
Germany ドイツ Switzerland スイス
Italy イタリア Egypt エジプト
Russia ロシア India インド
China 中国 Singapore シンガポール
Japan 日本 Korea 韓国
Australia オーストラリア Canada カナダ
The United States アメリカ Brazil ブラジル
name 名前 is〜です
I'm I amの短縮形
from（場所を示して）〜出身で，〜から
where どこで，どこに

**和訳**

My name is Mira. わたしの名前はミラです。/ I'm from India. わたしはインドの出身です。
Where are you from? あなたはどこの出身ですか。/ I'm from Brazil. ぼくはブラジルの出身です。

**留意点**

● 国際化教育の波は小学校にもおよんでいます。外国の名称もまんがや雑誌，アニメなどに現れますから，興味を示すでしょう。

● 日本の位置を示し，それぞれの国がどの位置にあるか確かめさせましょう。

● 固有名詞は大文字で始めます。

● Americaは，ふつうアメリカ大陸全体を指します。

● イギリスはグレートブリテン島のイングランド，スコットランド，ウェールズと，北部アイルランドから成ります。国全体を指す場合はGreat Britainを使います。Englandとはいいません。

● 「私の名前は〜です」というときは，My name is〜. を使います。
例 My name is Luka. （わたしの名前はルカです。）

● 「どこから，どこに」と場所をたずねるときは，文の始めにwhereを置きます。
例 Where are you from? （あなたはどこの出身ですか。）
——I am from China. （わたしは中国出身です。）

**LET'S TRY**

問題 1 My name is Carmen. I'm from Spain.
2 My name is Ivan. I'm from Russia.
3 My name is Kazuya. I'm from Okinawa.

## Lesson 10 My family わたしの家族

**語句**

family 家族 sister 姉，妹
brother 兄，弟 grandmother（grandma）祖母
grandfather（grandpa）祖父 father（dad）父
mother（mom）母 parents 両親
uncle おじ aunt おば
cousin いとこ son 息子
wife 妻 husband 夫
daughter 娘 this これは，これが
who だれ it それは

**和訳**

This is my brother, Akira. こちらはぼくの兄のあきらです。/ And this is my sister, Sayaka. そしてこちらはぼくの妹のさやかです。
Who is this? こちらはだれですか。/ It is my cousin, Naoto. ぼくのいとこのなおとです。

**留意点**

● 家族の名称を学びます。grandpa（祖父），grandma（祖母），dad（父），mom（母）は会話でよく使われます。

● 兄弟，姉妹の間では，名前で呼び合います。

● 「こちらは〜です」というときは，This is〜.を使います。

● 「だれ」と人をたずねるときは，文の始めにwhoを置きます。
例 Who is she? （彼女はだれですか。）
——She is Mami Koike. （彼女は小池真美です。）

● p.23のIt is my cousin, Naoto. のItは，Who is this? のthisを置きかえたものです。

**LET'S TRY**

問題 1 Who is this?
It's my brother, Akira.
2 Who is this?
It's you, Rika.
3 Who is this?
It's my mother.

## Lesson 11　Our house　わたしたちの家

**語句**

| | |
|---|---|
| our わたしたちの | garage ガレージ |
| car 車 | chimney えんとつ |
| roof 屋根 | shutter シャッター |
| gate 門 | step ふみ段 |
| intercom インターフォン | nameplate 表札 |
| flower bed 花だん | garden 庭 |
| pond 池 | lawn しばふ |
| wall かべ | fence フェンス |
| house 家 | that あれは，あれが |

**和訳**

This is my house. これはぼくの家です。

This is a pond. これは池です。/ That is a chimney. あれはえんとつです。

**留意点**

● インターフォンはintercomを使います。まちがえやすいので注意しましょう。

● 「これ(あれ)は～です」というときは，This(That) is ～. を使います。thisは話し手の近くにあるもの，thatは話し手からはなれたものを指します。

例　This is my pen.　(これはわたしのペンです。)
　　That is my pen.　(あれはわたしのペンです。)

● myとa(an)は同時に使いません。

例　This is a book.
　　(これは本です。)
　　This is my book.
　　(これはわたしの本です。)

**LET'S TRY**

問題　1　That is my car.
　　　2　This is a chimney.
　　　3　This is a roof.

## Lesson 12　In our house　わたしたちの家の中

**語句**

| | |
|---|---|
| in(場所を示して)～の中に | entrance 玄関 |
| stairs 階段 | dining room ダイニング |
| kitchen キッチン | living room 居間 |
| bedroom 寝室 | bathroom ふろ |
| toilet トイレ | yes はい |
| soap せっけん | shampoo シャンプー |
| rinse リンス | shower シャワー |
| mirror 鏡 | toothbrush 歯ブラシ |
| tissue ティッシュ | hair dryer ドライヤー |
| washing machine せんたく機 | slippers スリッパ |
| scale 体重計 | no いいえ |
| not ～でない，～しない | |

**和訳**

Is this a bathroom? これはふろですか。/ Yes, it is. はい，そうです。

Is that your shampoo? あれはあなたのシャンプーですか。/ No, it is not. いいえ，ちがいます。

**留意点**

● 屋内にある階段をstairs，屋外にある階段をstepsといいます。

● 「これ(あれ)は～ですか」というときは，This(That) is ～. のthis(that)とisの順番を入れかえます。

例　This is my bag.　(これはわたしのかばんです。)
　　Is this my bag?　(これはわたしのかばんですか。)

※　疑問文の最後には？(クエスチョンマーク)をつけます。

● 疑問文を話すときは，文の終わりを上げます。

● Is this(that)～？の文に答えるときは，this(that)をitに置きかえて，Yes, it is. またはNo, it is not. を使います。

例　Is this my bag?
　　――Yes, it is.　(はい，そうです。)
　　　　No, it is not.　(いいえ，ちがいます。)

※　否定の場合の答え方はNo, it isn't. が一般的ですが，ここではNo, it is not. を確実に覚えさせましょう。

**LET'S TRY**

問題　1　Is this your room?
　　　　 Yes, it is.
　　　2　Is that your toothbrush?
　　　　 No, it isn't.
　　　3　Is this our kitchen?
　　　　 Yes, it is.

## Lesson 13　Our living room　わたしたちの居間

**語句**

| | |
|---|---|
| air conditioner エアコン | TV(television) テレビ |
| telephone 電話 | photo 写真 |
| stereo ステレオ | computer コンピューター |
| printer プリンター | keyboard キーボード |
| picture 絵 | vacuum cleaner そうじ機 |
| cell phone けいたい電話 | floor ゆか |
| cushion クッション | newspaper 新聞 |
| remote control リモコン | table テーブル |
| magazine 雑誌 | vase 花びん |
| rug じゅうたん | light ライト |
| sofa ソファー | what 何 |
| it's it isの短縮形 | |

**和訳**

What is this? これは何ですか。/ It's a light. ライトです。

What is that? あれは何ですか。/ It's a picture. 絵です。

**留意点**

● 次のことばはまちがえやすいので注意しましょう。

エアコン　air conditioner
テレビ　TV(television)
リモコン　remote control

● ゆか全体にしくじゅうたんをcarpet，ゆかの一部にしくじゅうたんをrugといいます。

● 「これ(あれ)は何ですか」とたずねるときは，文の始めにwhatを置きます。

例　What is this?
　　(これは何ですか。)

● Is this～? / Is that～? の答えの文では，thisやthatをitに置きかえました。同じように，What is this? の答えの文でもthisをitに置きかえます。

例　What is this?
　　――It is a piano.　(ピアノです。)

● it'sはit isが短縮された形です。通常はこの形を使います。

**LET'S TRY**

問題　1　What's this?
　　　　 It's a rug.
　　　2　What's this?
　　　　 It's a telephone.
　　　3　What's this?
　　　　 It's a keyboard.

## Lesson 14　Our kitchen わたしたちの台所

**語句**

microwave oven 電子レンジ　oil 油
pepper こしょう　salt 塩
sink 流し　frying pan フライパン
pot なべ　gas stove ガスコンロ
refrigerator 冷蔵庫　cupboard たな
glass グラス　dish 大きい皿
plate 取り皿　spoon スプーン
fork フォーク　knife ナイフ
kettle やかん　tablecloth テーブルクロス
trash can ごみ箱　sugar 砂糖
cup カップ　teapot きゅうす
isn't　is not の短縮形　whose だれの
mine わたしのもの

**和訳**

This isn't my cup. これはぼくのカップではありません。/ It's my brother's. ぼくの兄のです。
Whose plate is this? これはだれの皿ですか。/ It's mine. ぼくのです。

**留意点**

● 次のことばはまちがえやすいので注意しましょう。
電子レンジ　microwave oven
ガスコンロ　gas stove
● cupboard(たな)の "p" は発音しません。注意しましょう。
● 平なべを pan，深いなべを pot といいます。
● 大皿を dish，１人用の皿を plate といいます。
● 「これ(あれ)は～ではありません」というときは，is のあとに not を置きます。
例　This is not my bag.
(これはわたしのかばんではありません。)
● 「だれの」ともち主をたずねるときは，文の始めに whose を置きます。
例　Whose book is this?　(これはだれの本ですか。)
———It's mine.　(それはわたしのです。)
Whose piano is that?　(あれはだれのピアノですか。)
———It's my sister's.　(それは姉のです。)
● 「～の，～のもの」というときは，名詞の語尾に -'s(アポストロフィーエス)をつけます。
例　Ken's bag　(健のかばん)
Rika's father　(里香のお父さん)

**LET'S TRY**

問題　1　Whose fork is this?
2　It's not sugar.  It's salt.
3　This isn't my spoon.  Whose spoon is this?

## Lesson 15　My room わたしの部屋

**語句**

room 部屋　curtain カーテン
CD シーディー
CD player シーディープレイヤー
camera カメラ　bookcase 本箱
globe 地球儀　desk 机
calendar カレンダー　book 本
bat バット　poster ポスター
chair いす　comic book まんがの本
album アルバム　glove グローブ
bag かばん　bed ベッド
pillow まくら　the その
on(場所を示して)～の上に，～に
then それなら　they それらは，彼らは
under(場所を示して)～の下に

**和訳**

Where is my glove? ぼくのグローブはどこですか。/ It's in the bag. かばんの中です。
Where is my bat? ぼくのバットはどこですか。/ It's on the chair. いすの上です。/ Where are my balls, then? では，ぼくのボールはどこですか。/ They are under the chair. いすの下です。

**留意点**

● 野球のグローブが glove[glʌ́v]，地球儀が globe[glóub]です。混同しやすいので注意しましょう。
● 「～はどこですか」と場所をたずねるときは，where を文の始めに置きます。答えるときは，単数の場合 It is(It's)～. を使い，複数の場合 They are～. を使います。
例　Where is my album?　(わたしのアルバムはどこですか。)
———It's on the desk.　(机の上です。)
Where are my CDs?
(わたしのシーディーはどこですか。)
———They are on the chair.　(いすの上です。)
● 場所を表す前置詞 in，on，under の学習をします。
例　It's in the box.　(箱の中です。)
It's on the cushion.　(クッションの上です。)
They are under the bed.　(ベッドの下です。)

**LET'S TRY**

問題　Where is my globe?
It's on the bookcase.
Where are my CDs, then?
They are in the bookcase.

## Lesson 16　In the country いなか

**語句**

country 郊外，いなか　woods 森
sky 空　temple 寺
bush やぶ　orchard 果樹園
expressway 高速道路　rice field 田
hill 丘　amusement park 遊園地
lake 湖　hotel ホテル
road 道　ball park 野球場
let's(さそいかけるときに)～しましょう
go 行く　to(行き先を示して)～へ
favorite 大好きな　place 場所
an １つの

**和訳**

Let's go to the lake. 湖へ行きましょう。
Where is your favorite place? あなたの大好きな場所はどこですか。/ It's an amusement park. 遊園地です。

**留意点**

● sky(空)は単独で使う場合に，the をとります。また，形容詞がつく場合はふつう a をとります。
例　The sky is blue.　(空は青い色をしています。)
We have a clear sky today.
(今日は空が晴れています。)
● 野球場は baseball stadium ともいいます。
● 「～しましょう」とさそいかけるときは，命令文の始めに Let's を置きます。
例　Let's go to the amusement park.
(遊園地へ行きましょう。)
Let's sing the song.　(その歌を歌いましょう。)
● 「大好きな」というときは，favorite を使います。
例　This is my favorite place.

（ここはわたしの大好きな場所です。）
What is your favorite color?
（あなたの大好きな色は何ですか。）

**LET'S TRY**

問題　1　Where is your favorite place?
　　　　It's a lake.
　　　2　Where is your favorite place?
　　　　It's a ball park.
　　　3　Where is your favorite place?
　　　　It's an orchard.

## Lesson 17　In the town 町の中

**語句**

| | |
|---|---|
| town 町 | station 駅 |
| museum 博物館，美術館 | |
| supermarket スーパーマーケット | |
| parking lot 駐車場 | |
| family restaurant ファミリーレストラン | |
| factory 工場 | bus stop バス停 |
| crosswalk 横断歩道 | park 公園 |
| vending machine 自動販売機 | school 学校 |
| police station 警察署 | post office 郵便局 |
| fire station 消防署 | |
| convenience store コンビニエンスストアー | |
| intersection 交差点 | bookstore 書店 |
| theater 劇場 | department store デパート |
| street 通り | traffic light 信号 |
| bank 銀行 | hospital 病院 |
| next となりに *next* to ～のとなりに | |
| front 正面 in *front* of ～の正面に | of（部分を示して）～の |

**和訳**

Where is a bank? 銀行はどこですか。/ It's next to the hospital. 病院のとなりです。/ Where is a museum? 博物館はどこですか。/ It's in front of the station. 駅の正面です。

**留意点**

● 交差点はcrossingともいいます。
● 「～のとなりに」というときは，next toを使い，「～の正面に」というときは，in front ofを使います。

**LET'S TRY**

問題　Where is the hospital?
　　　It's next to the theater.
　　　Where is the theater, then?
　　　It's next to the post office.

## Lesson 18　Fruits 果物

**語句**

| | |
|---|---|
| fruit 果物 | apple りんご |
| banana バナナ | orange オレンジ |
| cherry さくらんぼ | strawberry いちご |
| blueberry ブルーベリー | grapes ぶどう |
| grapefruit グレープフルーツ | lemon レモン |
| melon メロン | watermelon すいか |
| peach もも | fig いちじく |
| pear なし | persimmon かき |
| kiwi キウイ | mango マンゴー |
| pineapple パイナップル | chestnut くり |
| walnut くるみ | coconut ココナッツ |
| like 好きだ | |
| do（動詞とともに用いて現在形の否定文を作る） | |

**和訳**

I like apples. ぼくはりんごが好きです。
I do not like bananas. わたしはバナナが好きではありません。

**留意点**

● グレープは１つぶのぶどうのことです。１ふさのぶどうはa bunch of grapesといいます。
● 「わたしは～が好きです」というときは，I like ～. を使います。一般的な好き嫌いを表すとき，likeのあとに数えられる名詞が続く場合は，名詞を複数形にします。
　例　I like oranges.（わたしはオレンジが好きです。）
　　　I like orange juice.
　　　（わたしはオレンジジュースが好きです。）
● 「わたしは～が好きではありません」というときは，likeの前にdon'tを置きます。
　例　I <u>don't like</u> bananas.

**LET'S TRY**

問題　1　I like watermelons.
　　　2　I don't like lemons.
　　　3　I like walnuts.

## Lesson 19　Vegetables 野菜

**語句**

| | |
|---|---|
| vegetable 野菜 | carrot にんじん |
| onion たまねぎ | potato じゃがいも |
| cucumber きゅうり | lettuce レタス |
| tomato トマト | cabbage キャベツ |
| celery セロリ | corn とうもろこし |
| green pepper ピーマン | asparagus アスパラガス |
| broccoli ブロッコリー | parsley パセリ |
| radish ラディッシュ | pumpkin かぼちゃ |
| spinach ほうれん草 | turnip かぶ |
| beans 豆 | eggplant なす |
| okra オクラ | mushroom マッシュルーム |
| garlic にんにく | ginger しょうが |
| leek ねぎ | |
| do（動詞とともに用いて現在形の疑問文やその答えの文を作る） | |
| don't do notの短縮形 | |

**和訳**

Do you like carrots? あなたはにんじんが好きですか。/ Yes, I do. はい，好きです。
Do you like leeks? あなたはねぎが好きですか。/ No, I don't. いいえ，好きではありません。

**留意点**

● 「あなたは～が好きですか」というときは，文の始めにdoを置きます。
　例　Do you like oranges?
● lettuce（レタス），celery（セロリ），asparagus（アスパラガス），parsley（パセリ），spinach（ほうれん草），garlic（にんにく），ginger（しょうが）は数えられないので，複数形はありません。
　例　Do you like carrots?
　　　（あなたはにんじんが好きですか。）
　　　Do you like lettuce?
　　　（あなたはレタスが好きですか。）

**LET'S TRY**

問題　1　Do you like carrots?
　　　　Yes, I do.
　　　2　Do you like cabbages?
　　　　Yes, I do.
　　　3　Do you like garlic?
　　　　No, I don't.

## Lesson 20　Sports スポーツ

**語句**

| | |
|---|---|
| sport スポーツ | baseball 野球 |
| basketball バスケットボール | soccer サッカー |
| volleyball バレーボール | rugby ラグビー |
| softball ソフトボール | badminton バドミントン |
| tennis テニス | table tennis 卓球 |
| gymnastics 器械体操 | high jump 高とび |
| marathon マラソン | track and field 陸上競技 |
| weight lifting ウエイトリフティング | |
| boxing ボクシング | golf ゴルフ |
| bowling ボーリング | skating スケート |
| skiing スキー | skateboarding スケートボード |
| surfing サーフィン | swimming 水泳 |
| she 彼女は | often しばしば |
| play(遊び，スポーツ，楽器の演奏などを)する | |
| well うまく | but しかし，でも |
| he 彼は | does(do の 3 人称・単数・現在) |
| very とても，(否定文中で)あまり～でない | |

**和訳**

My sister likes tennis. わたしの姉はテニスが好きです。/ She often plays tennis. 彼女はしばしばテニスをします。

My brother plays soccer well. ぼくの兄はサッカーが上手です。/ But he does not play baseball very well. でも，彼は野球があまり上手ではありません。

**留意点**

● 主語が I，you 以外で，それが単数の場合は，動詞の語尾に -s または -es をつけます。

例　He likes swimming.　(彼は水泳が好きです。)

また，「～ではありません」というときは，do not の代わりに，does not を使います。そのとき動詞の語尾に -s，または -es はつけません。

例　My father does not play golf.
(わたしの父はゴルフをしません。)

● 「(スポーツを)する」というときは，play を使います。ただし，play は skating，skiing，swimming などには使えません。

例　I play baseball.　(わたしは野球をします。)
I go skating.　(わたしはスケートに行きます。)

● 否定文の very は，「あまり～でありません」という意味です。

例　He does not cook very well.
(彼は料理があまり上手ではありません。)

**LET'S TRY**

問題　1　Ken plays basketball well.
2　He doesn't play baseball very well.
3　Rika plays badminton well.

## Lesson 21　Instruments 楽器

**語句**

| | |
|---|---|
| instrument 楽器 | castanets カスタネット |
| harmonica ハーモニカ | recorder リコーダー |
| cymbals シンバル | tambourine タンバリン |
| triangle トライアングル | piano ピアノ |
| violin バイオリン | cello チェロ |
| bass ベース | drums ドラム |
| guitar ギター | saxophone サックス |
| clarinet クラリネット | flute フルート |
| trumpet トランペット | accordion アコーディオン |
| xylophone 木琴 | harp ハープ |
| the(楽器，用具などにつける) play *the* piano | |
| doesn't does not の短縮形 | |

**和訳**

Does your mother play the piano? あなたのお母さんはピアノをひきますか。/ Yes, she does. はい，ひきます。

Does your father play the guitar? あなたのお父さんはギターをひきますか。/ No, he doesn't. いいえ，ひきません。

**留意点**

● castanets(カスタネット)，cymbals(シンバル)，drums(ドラム)は，複数形で使います。

● 「(楽器を)演奏する」というときは，〈play＋the＋楽器〉を使います。

例　I play the piano.　(わたしはピアノをひきます。)

● Your mother plays the piano. を疑問文にするには，do の代わりに does を使います。そのとき，動詞の語尾に -s，-es はつけません。また，答えるときも does を使います。

例　Does your mother play the piano?
(あなたのお母さんはピアノをひきますか。)
――Yes, she does.　(はい，ひきます。)
No, she doesn't.　(いいえ，ひきません。)

**LET'S TRY**

問題　1　Does she play the piano?　Yes, she does.
2　Does he play the cymbals?　Yes, he does.
3　Does she play the drums?　No, she doesn't.

## Lesson 22　Our elementary school わたしたちの小学校

**語句**

| | |
|---|---|
| school building 校舎 | gym 体育館 |
| swing ブランコ | pool プール |
| playground 運動場 | jungle gym ジャングルジム |
| track トラック | bar てつぼう |
| nurse's room 保健室 | principal's room 校長室 |
| teachers' room 職員室 | computer room コンピュータールーム |
| library 図書室 | elementary school 小学校 |
| we わたしたちは | have もっている |
| Japanese 国語 | math 算数，数学 |
| social studies 社会 | science 理科 |
| music 音楽 | fine arts 図画工作 |
| PE 体育 | English 英語 |
| what's what is の短縮形 | subject 教科 |

**和訳**

This is our elementary school. これはわたしたちの小学校です。/ We have a computer room. コンピュータールームがあります。

What's your favorite subject? あなたの大好きな教科は何ですか。/ It's PE. 体育です。

**留意点**

● 「職員室」は teachers' room です。-s で終わる複数名詞を「～の」という形にするときは，'(アポストロフィー)だけをつけます。

例　a girls' high school　(女子高校)

**LET'S TRY**

問題　1　My name is Seiji.　I like music.
2　I'm Maki.　I like science.

## Lesson 23　Our classroom わたしたちの教室

**語句**

| | | |
|---|---|---|
| clock 時計 | speaker スピーカー | |
| class schedule 時間割 | | map 地図 |
| blackboard 黒板 ※黒板は chalkboard ともいいます。 | | |
| chalk チョーク | notebook ノート | textbook 教科書 |
| dictionary 辞書 | pencil えんぴつ | |

mechanical pencil シャープペンシル pen ペン
eraser 消しゴム ruler じょうぎ scissors はさみ
paste のり stapler ホッチキス paint 絵の具
crayons クレヨン there *there* is(are)〜がある
classroom 教室 many たくさんの

**和訳**

There is a blackboard in our classroom. わたしたちの教室には黒板があります。
There are many books on the desk. 机の上にはたくさんの本があります。

**留意点**

● はさみ(scissors)は常に複数形で使います。
● 次のことばはまちがえやすいので注意しましょう。
シャープペンシル　mechanical pencil
ホッチキス　stapler
● 「〜があります」というときは，There is〜. / There are〜. を使います。１つのものを表すにはThere is〜. を，２つ以上のものを表すにはThere are〜. を使います。
例　There is a book in the bag.
(かばんの中に１冊の本があります。)
There are two pens on the piano.
(ピアノの上に２本のペンがあります。)

**LET'S TRY**

問題　There is a desk in the room.
There are many pencils on the desk.

## Lesson 24　The sea 海

**語句**

beach 海岸 seagull かもめ
beach umbrella ビーチパラソル shell 貝
wave 波 crab かに goggles ゴーグル
inner tube うきわ swimsuit 水着 turtle かめ
whale くじら palm tree ココヤシ lighthouse 灯台
island 島 octopus たこ shark さめ
squid いか dolphin いるか yacht ヨット
boat ボート shrimp えび ship 船
any いくらか sea 海 some いくつかの

**和訳**

Is there a lighthouse on the beach? 海岸に灯台がありますか。/ No there isn't. いいえ，ありません。
Are there any ships in the sea? 海には船が何そうかありますか。/ Yes. はい。/ There are some ships. 何そうかの船があります。

**留意点**

● ビーチパラソルはbeach umbrellaといいます。まちがえやすいので注意しましょう。
● 「〜がありますか」とたずねるときは，There is(are)〜. のthereとis(are)の順番を入れかえます。
例　Is there a book?　(本がありますか。)
● Is(Are) there〜? の文に答えるときは，Yes, there is(are). かNo, there isn't(aren't). を使います。
例　Is there a violin on the piano?
——Yes, there is. / No, there isn't.
● 「いくらか，いくつか」という場合，ふつうの文(肯定文)ではsome，疑問文や否定文ではanyを使います。
例　There are some books on the desk.
(机の上には本が何冊かあります。)
Are there any pencils on the desk?
(机の上にはえんぴつが何本かありますか。)

**LET'S TRY**

問題　1　Is there a boat on the ship?
Yes, there is.
2　Are there any palm trees on the island?
Yes, there are.
3　Are there any seagulls on the beach?
No, there aren't.

## Lesson 25　Mountains 山

**語句**

mountain 山 bear くま monkey さる
tent テント chipmunk りす fire 火
backpack リュックサック
barbecue バーベキュー river 川
stone 石 bridge 橋 owl ふくろう
spider くも cicada せみ dragonfly とんぼ
woodpecker きつつき snake へび
deer しか skunk スカンク fox きつね

**和訳**

How many bears are there? 何頭のくまがいますか。/ Two bears. ２頭です。

**留意点**

● 「リュックサック」はbackpackといいます。まちがえやすいので注意しましょう。
● 「いくつありますか(いますか)」というときは，How many〜are there? を使います。
例　How many apples are there?
(りんごはいくつありますか。)

**LET'S TRY**

問題　How many monkeys are there in the tent?
Four monkeys.

## Lesson 26　At the zoo 動物園

**語句**

at(場所を示して)〜で zoo 動物園
giraffe きりん zebra しまうま ostrich だちょう
elephant ぞう lion ライオン cheetah チーター
gorilla ゴリラ chimpanzee チンパンジー
alligator わに hippopotamus かば rhinoceros さい
camel らくだ panda パンダ tiger とら
flamingo フラミンゴ peacock くじゃく
koala コアラ kangaroo カンガルー penguin ペンギン
sea lion あしか big 大きい small 小さい
has(haveの３人称・単数・現在) long 長い
short 短い

**和訳**

Gorillas are big.ゴリラは大きいです。/ Chimpanzees are small.チンパンジーは小さいです。
A flamingo has long legs. フラミンゴの脚は長いです。/ A penguin has short legs. ペンギンの脚は短いです。

**留意点**

● 形容詞には，次のような２とおりの使い方があります。
例　This stone is big. この石は大きい。
This is a big stone. これは大きい石です。
● 「ゴリラは大きいです」のように，ゴリラ一般について表す場合には，「Gorillas(複数形)」または「A gorilla(AまたはAn＋単数形)」がよく使われます。
例　Gorillas are big. / A gorilla is big.

**LET'S TRY**

問題　1　I'm an elephant. I like apples.
2　I'm a chimpanzee. I like bananas.
3　I'm a sea lion. I like fish.

## Lesson 27　On the farm 農場

**語句**

| | |
|---|---|
| farm 農場 | swallow つばめ |
| pigeon はと | dog 犬 |
| cat ねこ | pig ぶた |
| crow からす | sparrow すずめ |
| butterfly ちょう | rabbit うさぎ |
| bee はち | hen めんどり |
| mole もぐら | horse 馬 |
| sheep 羊 | cow 牛 |
| goat やぎ | swan 白鳥 |
| duck かも，あひる | mouse ねずみ |
| frog かえる | what どんな |
| animal 動物 | |

**和訳**

What animal do you like? あなたはどんな動物が好きですか。/ I like dogs. わたしは犬が好きです。

What animal do you have? あなたはどんな動物を飼っていますか。/ I have a rabbit. わたしはうさぎを飼っています。

**留意点**

● cow(牛)，pig(ぶた)，hen(にわとり)は動物のことです。肉はそれぞれbeef，pork，chickenといいます。

● whatはWhat is this? のように単独で使うことも，What time is it now? のように名詞を続けて使うこともできます。

例　What is your name?
（あなたの名前は何ですか。）
What fruit do you like best?
（どんな果物がいちばん好きですか。）

**LET'S TRY**

問題　1　I have two dogs.
2　I have many cows and pigs.
3　I like cats.  But they don't like me.

## Lesson 28　Time and the days of the week 時間と曜日

**語句**

| | | |
|---|---|---|
| week 週 | thirteen 13 | fourteen 14 |
| fifteen 15 | sixteen 16 | seventeen 17 |
| eighteen 18 | nineteen 19 | twenty 20 |
| thirty 30 | forty 40 | fifty 50 |
| sixty 60 | seventy 70 | eighty 80 |
| ninety 90 | hundred 100 | twenty-one 21 |

| | |
|---|---|
| time 時間 | it(時，日などを指す) |
| now 今 | morning 朝 |
| afternoon 午後 | night 夜 |
| noon 正午 | midnight 真夜中 |
| Sunday 日曜日 | Monday 月曜日 |
| Tuesday 火曜日 | Wednesday 水曜日 |
| Thursday 木曜日 | Friday 金曜日 |
| Saturday 土曜日 | day 日，1日 |
| today 今日 | |

**和訳**

What time is it now? 今何時ですか。/ It's two thirty. 2時30分です。

What day is it today?今日は何曜日ですか。/ It's Friday. 金曜日です。

**留意点**

● 21，22，23，…は，twenty-one，twenty-two，twenty-three，…となります。

● 今の時刻をたずねるときは，What time is it now? を，今日の曜日をたずねるときは，What day is it today? を使います。2つの文の主語のitは特に意味をもたず，ばくぜんと時や日を表しています。

● 曜日の名称は大文字で書き始めます。

**LET'S TRY**

問題　1　What time is it now?
It's ten.
2　What day is it today?
It's Sunday.
3　What time is it now?
It's five forty.

## Lesson 29　Seasons 季節

**語句**

| | |
|---|---|
| spring 春 | March 3月 |
| April 4月 | May 5月 |
| summer 夏 | June 6月 |
| July 7月 | August 8月 |
| fall 秋 | September 9月 |
| October 10月 | November 11月 |
| winter 冬 | December 12月 |
| January 1月 | February 2月 |
| season 季節 | best いちばん |
| when いつ | birthday 誕生日 |
| in(月，季節などを示して)～に | |

**和訳**

What season do you like best? どの季節がいちばん好きですか。/ I like summer best. 夏がいちばん好きです。

When is your birthday? あなたの誕生日はいつですか。/ It's in July. 7月です。

**留意点**

● 月の名称は大文字で書き始めます。

● 「どんな～がいちばん好きですか」とたずねるときは，「What ～ do you like best?」といいます。

例　What color do you like best?
（あなたは何色がいちばん好きですか。）
——I like red best.
（赤がいちばん好きです。）

● 「いつ」と時をたずねるときは文の始めにwhenを置きます。

例　When do you play soccer?
（あなたはいつサッカーをしますか。）
——Every Sunday.
（毎週日曜日です。）

● 「(～月)に」というときはinを使い，「(～月～日)に」というときはonを使います。

例　My birthday is in October.
My birthday is on October 9.

**LET'S TRY**

問題　1　What season do you like best?
I like spring best.
2　What season do you like best?
I like fall best.
3　When is your birthday?
It's in February.

## Lesson 30　Flowers and Trees 花と木

**語句**

| | |
|---|---|
| tree 木 | cherry blossoms さくら |
| pansy パンジー | tulip チューリップ |
| dandelion たんぽぽ | azalea つつじ |
| violet すみれ | carnation カーネーション |

lily ゆり
rose バラ
hydrangea あじさい
morning glory あさがお
sunflower ひまわり
cactus サボテン
cosmos コスモス
dahlia ダリア
pine tree 松
bamboo 竹
which どちらが
better もっと
or それとも
flower 花

**和訳**

Which do you like better, tulips or roses? チューリップとバラではどちらのほうが好きですか。/ I like roses better. バラの方が好きです。

What color is the flower? その花は何色ですか。/ It's yellow. 黄色です。

**留意点**

● 「どちら」と２つのうちの１つを選ばせるときは，文の始めにwhich を置きます。

例 Which is your bag, this or that?
（どちらがあなたのかばんですか，これですか，それともあれですか。）
――― This is my bag.
（これがわたしのかばんです。）

また，「AとBではどちらが好きですか」とたずねるときは，better(よりよく，より多く)を使って次のように表現します。

例 Which do you like better, dogs or cats?
（あなたは犬とねこではどちらが好きですか。）
――― I like cats better.
（ねこのほうが好きです。）

**LET'S TRY**

問題 1 Which do you like better, pansies or tulips?
2 Which do you like better, carnations or sunflowers?
3 Which do you like better, pine trees or bamboos?

## Lesson 31 Vehicles 乗り物

**語句**

vehicle 乗り物
train 電車
subway 地下鉄
bus バス
taxi タクシー
monorail モノレール
tricycle 三輪車
bicycle 自転車
motorcycle オートバイ
balloon 気球
helicopter ヘリコプター
airplane 飛行機
ambulance 救急車
police car パトロールカー
truck トラック
fire engine 消防車
garbage truck せいそう車
bulldozer ブルドーザー
crane truck クレーン車
work 仕事
by （手段を示して）～で
how どのように *How* do you go to school? あなたはどのように学校へ行きますか。

**和訳**

My mother goes to work by train. わたしの母は電車で仕事へ行きます。

How do you go to school? あなたはどのようにして学校へ行きますか。/ By bus. バスで行きます。

**留意点**

● アメリカでは，bike は自転車のことです。まちがえやすいので注意しましょう。

● My mother goes to work by train. のように，「(乗り物)で」というときは，〈by＋無冠詞の名詞〉を使います。

例 I go to school by bus.
（わたしはバスで学校に行きます。）
Do you go to work by bicycle?
（あなたは自転車で仕事に行きますか。）

※ 歩いて行く場合には，on foot を使います。

例 He goes to school on foot.
（彼は歩いて学校へ行きます。）

● 「どのように」と手段や方法を表すときはHow を文の始めに置きます。

例 How do I go there?
（そこへはどのように行けばよいのですか。）
How do you say "bicycle" in Japanese?
（"bicycle" は日本語で何といいますか。）

**LET'S TRY**

問題 1 How do you go to work?
By train.
2 How does he go to school?
By bicycle.
3 How does she go to the station?
By bus.

## Lesson 32 Jobs 仕事

**語句**

job 仕事
baseball player 野球選手
actor 俳優，女優
singer 歌手
pilot パイロット
flight attendant スチュワード，スチュワーデス
astronaut 宇宙飛行士
cartoonist まんが家
painter 画家
writer 作家
carpenter 大工
cook コック
farmer 農業従事者
doctor 医者
nurse 看護師
scientist 科学者
fire fighter 消防士
police officer 警察官
teacher 先生
lawyer 弁護士
politician 政治家
office worker 事務所で働く人
want *want* to… ～したい
be am, is, are の原形

**和訳**

My father is a doctor. ぼくの父は医者です。/ My mother is an office worker. ぼくの母は事務所で働いています。

What do you want to be? あなたは何になりたいですか。/ I want to be a baseball player. ぼくは野球選手になりたいです。

**留意点**

● 子ども達が関心を示す職業ばかりですね。ここにあげたことばはすべて男性にも女性にも用いられます。

● 「～したい」というときは，〈want＋to＋動詞の原形〉を使います。

例 I want to play soccer.
（わたしはサッカーをしたいです。）
I want to eat bananas.
（わたしはバナナを食べたいです。）
Do you want to know about koalas?
（あなたはコアラのことを知りたいですか。）
Do you want to read this magazine?
（あなたはこの雑誌を読みたいですか。）

● What do you want to be? のbe は，am, is, are の原形です。ここでは，「～になる」という意味を表しています。

例 He will be a good actor.
（彼はよい役者になるでしょう。）

**LET'S TRY**

問題 1 I am a painter.
2 I want to be a singer.
3 I am a fire fighter.

## Lesson 33　Space 宇宙

**語句**

space 宇宙　shooting star 流れ星
rocket ロケット
space shuttle スペースシャトル
moon 月　Milky Way 天の川
alien エイリアン　satellite 人工衛星
star 星　UFO 空飛ぶ円盤
sun 太陽　rainbow にじ
wind 風　thunder 雷
snow 雪　rain 雨
cloud 雲　Earth 地球
interested be *interested* in ～に興味をもっている
much たくさんの very *much* とても
little a *little* 少しは

**和訳**

Are you interested in the moon? あなたは月に興味がありますか。/ Yes, very much. はい，とてもあります。
Are you interested in aliens? あなたはエイリアンに興味がありますか。/ Yes, a little. はい，少しあります。

**留意点**

● 宇宙や空中にあるものを集めました。the moon(月)，the Milky Way(天の川)，the sun(太陽)，the sky(空)，the Earth(地球)のように，1つしかないものは，冠詞theをとります。ただし，a full moon(満月)，a blue sky(青い空)のように，形容詞をともなうとaがつくものもあります。

●「～に興味があります」というときは，〈is, am, are＋interested＋in〉という形を使います。inのあとに数えられる名詞が続く場合は，名詞を複数形にします。

例　I am interested in music.
　(わたしは音楽に興味があります。)
　Are you interested in sports?
　(あなたはスポーツに興味がありますか。)

**LET'S TRY**

問題　1　I'm interested in space.
　2　Are you interested in rainbows?
　3　I'm not interested in UFOs.

## Lesson 34　High and low 高いと低い

**語句**

high 高い　low 低い
heavy 重い　light ①軽い②明るい
thick 厚い　thin うすい
deep 深い　shallow 浅い
right 右の　left 左の
dark 暗い　hard 固い
soft やわらかい　clean きれいな
dirty きたない　cold 冷たい
hot 熱い　new 新しい
old 古い　fast 速い
slow 遅い　good よい
bad 悪い

**和訳**

This mountain is low. この山は低い。/ That mountain is high. あの山は高い。

**留意点**

● 反対の意味を表す形容詞をあつかいます。

● p.70の例文のように，イラストを英語で表現させましょう。

例　This stone is heavy.
　(この石は重い。)
　This book is thin.
　(この本はうすい。)
　This pool is deep.
　(このプールは深い。)

● Lesson 26で学んだように，This is a low mountain. と，名詞の前に形容詞を置く形の文も練習させましょう。

**LET'S TRY**

問題　1　My bed is cold.
　2　My bath is deep.
　3　My room is dark.

## Lesson 35　My day 1日の生活

**語句**

get ① *get* up 起きる ② *get* to 着く
wash 洗う　comb (かみを)とかす
put *put* on (服を)着る　eat 食べる
breakfast 朝食　brush ブラシでみがく
teeth tooth(歯)の複数形　leave 出発する
home ①家を ②家へ　listen *listen* to ～を聞く
raise もち上げる *raise* a hand 手をあげる
lunch 昼食　talk 話す
with (相手を示して)～と　friend 友達
clean そうじをする　return もどる
watch じっと見る　video game テレビゲーム
dinner 夕食　help 手伝う
do する　homework 宿題
take *take* a bath ふろに入る　bath 入浴
go *go* to bed ねる　at (時間を示して)～に

**和訳**

I get up at 7. わたしは7時に起きます。
What time do you eat dinner? 何時に夕食を食べますか。/ At 6. 6時です。

**留意点**

● 1日の生活を表すことばをあつかいます。I, Youを主語にして口頭練習をしましょう。

● I get up at 7. のように「～時に」というときは，前置詞atを使います。

例　I eat breakfast at 7.
　(わたしは7時に朝食を食べます。)
　Do you leave home at 8?
　(あなたは8時に家を出ますか。)
　——Yes, I do.
　(はい，そうです。)

●「何時に～しますか」というときは，What time ～? を使います。

例　What time do you eat lunch?
　(あなたは何時に昼食を食べますか。)
　——At 12.　(12時です。)
　What time does your father return home?
　(あなたのお父さんは何時に家へ帰ってきますか。)
　——At 7.　(7時です。)

**LET'S TRY**

問題　1　What time do you go to bed?
　At 10.
　2　What time do you get to school?
　At 8.
　3　What time do you eat lunch?
　At 12.